MW01194317

The Sacred

Myths and Rites

of the

Madrians

Edited by Philip P Jackson

Hardback Edition August 2009

ISBN 978-1-4092-9547-1

Contents

THE CREATION

AND THE

CRYSTAL TABLET

ISSUED UNDER THE HAND OF THE GODDESS BY

Lux Madriana

THE
CREATION

THE
CRYSTAL TABLET

INTRODUCTION

Almost every line of the sacred Mythos contains such depths of inspiration that it cries out for a volume of commentary. Even so, the sisters concerned with issuing this edition feel that the words of our Lady revealed for the first time in many centuries, should stand alone, unvarnished by any human words.

Nevertheless, we have felt it necessary to include this brief preface to the Divine Truth in its modern English form, which may assist the modern reader in understanding it. If the reader does not feel our words to be of help, let her freely ignore them and pass directly to the real matter of these books, which is (quite literally) of infinitely greater importance.

One question in connection with The Creation and the Mythos of the Divine Maid which may trouble the modern reader is: "Did these events really happen and, if so, where and when?"

Here it is important to realize that Divine Myth gives us an image of Realities which in the fullest sense are beyond our comprehension. Physicists tell us that the smallest units of matter behave at once like particles and waves. In normal life, of course, this would be nonsense. A thing cannot at once be a particle, like a piece of chalk or cheese and a wave, like sound or a ripple on a pond. But through microscopic equipment

3

we are made aware of a world so different that our minds can make no real sense of it. And if we find such things on other levels of our own physical world, how strange and incomprehensible must be the spiritual world beyond space and time?

When we describe something as "at once like a particle and like a wave", we are not saying what it is really like (for we have neither words nor ideas which can grasp the reality of such things). We are simply taking two ideas which we can understand (particles and waves) and using them to point to a reality which we cannot.

In a way the Mythos is like that, for it is pointing toward an unknowable Reality. But it is not just a fallible human attempt to understand something which can never truly be understood. The Mythos is a divine paradigm, so perfect that when we read it with faith we gain a real knowledge of that which can in no other way be known. And it is a knowledge which does not stop at the conscious mind, but floods every level of our understanding with Divine Light.

To answer our original question directly: the events of the Mythos are real happenings. They take place on the Pleroma. The Pleroma is the highest level of being, beyond space and time; only on the Pleroma can an event have absolute reality. These Divine Events are at the base of all other existence. We cannot say that they have happened or that they will happen, or even that they are happening (though in a way that is closer to the truth). We can only say that they Happen. The creation of the world by the Mother, and its redemption by Her Daughter are the Absolute Events which underlie and make possible all other events. They are the condition of existence.

The Crystal Tablet is not a myth in this sense. Legend has it that at the beginning of time, the laws of life were inscribed upon a tablet of pure crystal. There are other Divine moral teachings, notably the inspired collection of the teachings of the Daughter. But within the Crystal Tablet is contained the gem of all moral teaching.

II

The words of the Mythos are the words of the Goddess. Human minds have created no part of it, but have only acted as channels through which the Divine authorship might flow. Nor is any part of the Mythos new. These things have been revealed to humanity at the dawn of time; and whenever the true worship of the Goddess is practised, She again reveals Her eternal truths.

When Her true religion is not practised and Her Truth is suppressed, religion must continue with only a pale and diluted form of the eternal revelation. The Creation is the pure essence which stands behind all other creation myths. In every later story of the death and resurrection of Deity can be found echoes of the Mythos of the Divine Maid. These echoes can sustain a religion for centuries; for they are echoes of pure Truth.

You hold that Truth in your hands. A Truth so deep that a lifetime of meditation will not cease to unfold new depths of meaning. A Truth which will pass through your conscious mind and permeate every level of your being, until it reaches that part of your eternal soul which has herself witnessed the sacred Events of the Mythos. For unlike all other religions, the religion of the Goddess teaches nothing. It only reminds the soul of those things which, in her deepest recesses, she knows already.

Your personal fate has led you into the possession of this book. Keep it beside you, for its words are living words, and they will be a source of comfort and inspiration when all other sources have failed.

THE CREATION

CHAPTER 1

Before and beyond all things is the Mistress of All Things, and when nothing was, She was. 2 And having no solid place that Her feet might rest upon, She divided the sea from the sky, and made a dance of solitary splendour upon the created deeps. 3 And She was pure force or energy, and therefore pure delight; and the crashing of the waves was the overflowing of Her joy. 4 And the white force of Her superabundant joy grew so great that it must take shape in laughter; and Her laughter was the shape of all things. 5 For each peal of Her voice became a silver fragment, broken from the Whole and yet complete in itself. And She loved each fragment with the joy of Her being, and Her hands knew cunning. 6 And She stretched forth Her hands and gave a shape to each fragment, and no one was like any other. 7 And She parted the vasty waters that there might be a place to set them down.

And She laughed.

8 And each fragment was filled with Her delight, and therefore was living. And some grew in the deep earth, and were plants and trees; some ran about the

ground or flew above it; and those first-made that had no place to be set down became the fishes and creatures of the sea. And every thing was silver.

And She laughed.

9 And at the edges, where the waters had been parted, they lay still and shallow; and there She cast Her gaze. And She saw an image of Herself, all suffused in the light of love and energy. And She laughed. 10 And as She laughed, the image rose up from the water and stood before Her. And this was the first of Her daughters. And She was filled with love for Her, and therefore was the first creature of spirit. 11 And she knew cunning, and she ran about the earth with love of all things, giving a name to every thing and creature, each in the order that She had shaped them.

12 And the Mistress of All Things was filled with delight, and ran laughing through the forests of the earth. 13 And every peal of Her voice became the image of a silver fragment of Her Spirit. 14 And the trees and rivers were filled with nymphs and every kind of sprite. And all were Her daughters. And Her love for each was inexhaustible, for each was a reflection of some boundless fragment of Her unbounded Spirit. 15 And all their multitude did not exhaust the number of the fragments of Her Spirit. 16 And to each was given the governance of some earthly thing.

CHAPTER TWO

But one there was that had not been shaped by Her, and that was not Her daughter, nor a creature of spirit. But he was the space between the fragments and the nothingness that had been before things were. He had not energy nor delight, but only weight. He had not shape but could only coil and uncoil himself about the things that were. He was the Snake, and was not silver, but black.

2 The Snake hated all things that had become, and hated the separation of the waters and the sky. He hated light and energy, desiring all to be darkness and nothingness.

3 And when the world had lived a time in joy (though what that time was none can say, for there were neither days nor nights, nor moons to tell the month), the Snake came to the first of the daughters of the Mistress of All things, and coiled about her feet and spoke to her:

4 First of the daughters of creation, you have lived in a time that cannot be counted, and have run for all that time in superfluity of energy, and have never known the sweetness of rest. Only embrace me and you shall have rest.

5 A long time she listened to the words of the Snake. She did not know what rest might be, but knew that it was not of Her. 6 And yet so enticingly did the Snake speak of the sweetness of rest, surpassing all delight, that at last she threw herself down and embraced him. 7 And because she was suffused with the delight of the Mistress of All Things, the Snake immediately took on shape. 8 And his shape was like to hers, but his body was filled with weight, and was barren, for being not a creature of spirit, he had not the power of creation.

9 And at once she became tired with all the outpouring of her energy, for her energy was no longer boundless. 10 And she desired to rest, but could not rest. And she spoke to the Snake, saying: Snake, what must I do now? 11 And the Snake said: First daughter of creation, you must go to the Mistress of All Things and ask Her to make the world dark that you may rest. 12 And so she asked that of Her, and She darkened the world for a period that Her daughter might rest. And this was the first night.

13 But when the darkness came, the Snake called to the waters and said: Waters, it is dark once more as it was in the beginning, and now you may come together, and all will be nothingness again. 14 And the waters heard him and began to flood the earth, and many were the creatures destroyed in that flood.

15 But the Mistress of All Things saw this and descended to the earth, placing Her heel upon the head of the Snake and bruising him. 16 And She flung the waters into the air that they might fall harmlessly to the earth in small drops. And this was the first rain.

CHAPTER THREE

And as the rain fell, the light came again, and a rainbow appeared in the sky, shedding its light upon all things. 2 And whereas all things had been silver, now they took on every hue and colour, and the world was beautiful; but it was not so beautiful as it had formerly been.

3 And She said to Her daughter: what you have done may not be undone, for you have acted with My Spirit, and henceforth shall time be divided into day and night that you may rest. 4 But I shall keep watch in the heavens by night, and there shall be a silver light that there may never be complete darkness. 5 By this shall I govern the movements if the waters, that the earth may never again be flooded. And when you look upon this light, you will remember the time when all things were silver.

6 The snake shall keep the form that you have given him, and you shall be set in governance over him; but remember that he will ever attempt to beguile and destroy you as he has this night.

7 I shall not live as close to you as before, but still I shall pour blessings upon you, and you may give Me gifts – not in every moment as before, for you have learned to tire, but My light shall give you signs in this matter.

8 And the Mistress of All Things withdrew Herself into the sky, until She seemed but a slender crescent of light. 9 And the first daughter of creation fell to her knees and wept. And these were the first tears shed upon the whole of the earth.

THE CRYSTAL TABLET

Existence is a web of tapestry.

2 A web is a pattern of many crossroads connected by short paths.

3 Some crossroads are the intersection of many paths, some but a few. Some are great and some are small. Each path has its own colour.

4 Every crossroads is a choice, and every choice has a spiritual meaning.

5 In each turning we choose either to come closer to Perfection or else to move away from Her.

6 In the first way the soul perfects herself in beauty; in the second she grows duller and more coarse.

7 In the first way she learns happiness even in dearth, and gathers riches of the spirit; in the second she learns pain even amid opulence, and the spirit walks in rags.

8 Where lead the paths? The first to the foot of the Celestial throne; the second to the dark gates of the realm of death.

9 How shall the soul know her direction?

10 As in the world of matter there are four fixed points by which the corporeal vessel may know its course, so, in the compass of the spirit, are there three to guide the soul.

11 The first is Life, or Wholeness, the light of the Absolute; the second is Light, or Energy, the light of the Mother; the third and gentlest light is Love, the light of our Saviour, the Maid.

Life is the life of the spirit – the first principle; beyond being and unbeing. Life Was before existence. Life is the cause of existence.

13 How shall the soul live in Life?

14 Let her realise the truth of her self and the Truth of the Absolute. Let her know that her life is beyond even her existence, that the Absolute Life, the Life of the Goddess, is beyond all existence.

15 Let her not be held from herself or her Goddess by any thing that exists, for all the things that are have come from nothing and to nothing shall return. But the Divine Life, and her life within it, Was ever and shall ever Be, though time itself shall only last a space.

16 Let her not trust the ground her feet are set upon and doubt the Ground upon which that ground stands. Rather let her doubt the sea, the sky, the fingers of her hand and the breath of her mouth; for all these things may be illusions, as in some sense they are.

17 But let her know Life Divine as the Truth beyond truth and the Faith beyond faith and doubt.

Light is pure force, or energy, or delight. It is the joy of the Goddess, and Her breath and Spirit.

19 Light is the outpouring of Life into existence. All things that exist come from Life; they are made and sustained by Light.

20 Though an existing thing appear never so solid, yet its body is made of light. All material things are but consolidated force; and the vibration of force is the whole of their being.

21 Yet material things are far from the Source of Light. They have become subject to consolidation and restriction.

22 Pure light knows no bounds, but is perfect joy, and breathes its own perfection.

23 How shall the soul approach to Light?

24 Let her make her every act a resplendent creation, and let every outpouring of her energy be a well-made gift for her Lady. Let her not fall into dullness, but be ever creating herself anew in the delight of her energy.

25 Let her not seek for reward, but only for her own perfection; thus shall the action itself become perfect. Let her turn from the transient and find delight in the Eternal.

26 For every earthly action is the shadow of some higher form; and the soul must choose whether in her act

she shall approach that form, or sink form it into deeper shadows and the morass of illusion.

27 She who rejects the light of the Spirit in this world shall, beyond death, be plunged into darkness and the confusion of bodiless echoes.

28 But every act that is performed in dedication to the Mother is an expression of the soul's true self, and loosens the chains of her bondage.

29 If the soul live in Light, no thing shall be impossible to her, for her will shall become one with the will of our Lady.

Love is the force of harmony by which all existence is made possible.

31 For the perfect existence of the Spirit, its very nature is Love. The pure soul is in harmony with the Goddess and with her self and with all things.

32 And for the existence that has fallen from perfection; truly it is the music of Divine harmony which sustains it in the motion of its wholeness.

33 It is Love that holds the drop of dew pendent upon a blade of grass, neither flowing forth in watery profusion, but swelling within the unseen urn of its brief harmony.

34 It is Love that holds the stars within their courses, and all the worlds of the immeasurable cosmos within the harmony of the celestial music.

35 Truly, all the cycles of the times and the seasons; all the rhythms of the soul and of the mind and of the body: truly all these flow from the love of our Lady the Maid, that creation may not decompose, each several member flying away into black eternal chaos.

36 For light is the essence and Love is the form. And it is by Love that the essence of a tree remains a tree. Else might it as well become a rushing wind or a forkéd lightning flash.

37 How shall the soul attain to Love?

38 Let her open herself to every creature in compassion and in care.

39 Let her seek to do no harm to any being.

40 Let her love extend even to those who do her hurt; and let her seek to understand them.

41 For perfect love is perfect knowledge and perfect knowledge is perfect love.

42 Let her know that no creature gains good for herself by any harmful act; for every stone returns to she that throws it in the fullness of time. And the shaft that her hand releases shall fly a thousand years until it cleave her heart.

43 But she that does a kindly action shall be thrice blessed.

44 Once in the doing of it; for the hand of the Goddess shall rest upon her.

45 Once in the raising of her soul upon the path toward her Lady.

46 And once in the deed itself; for every rose plucked and sent forth shall come as a gift to her when her heart is weary, and every cup of wine that she gives to another shall quench the thirst of her own lips in the fullness of time.

47. She who gives succour to those who have need prepares a place of safe repose for her soul. And she who turns no creature away surrounds her soul with beautiful things.

48 For the soul that grows in Love grows ever more beautiful, but the soul that turns from Love is repellent of aspect.

49 Let the soul know before all that the greatest love is the love of the Goddess, and from this love all other loves flow.

50 Let her open herself to her Lady that she may come as a perfect love for Her. Let her learn of the Goddess that eternal Love which is the Goddess.

51 And she who loves her Lady in perfection shall have perfect love of all Her creatures, even as She.

52 For this is the Love that is perfect knowledge, and the knowledge that is perfect Love.

THE MYTHOS

OF THE

DIVINE MAID

ISSUED UNDER THE HAND OF THE GODDESS BY

Lux Madriana

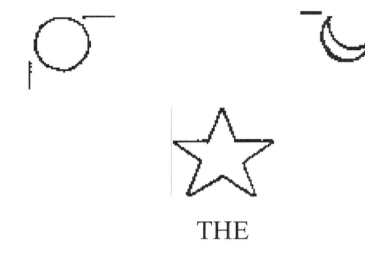

THE

MYTHOS

OF THE

DIVINE
MAID

CHAPTER I

When the first night had come upon world, the Mistress of All Things stood alone once more, as She had in the beginning. 2 For a terrible abyss had opened to lie between the world and She, and Her creatures could not look upon Her brightness.

3 And She stood in contemplation upon the waters of the first darkness; like a great Dove upon the waters She brooded 4 And She became absorbed within Her and communed with Her own Self; and Her light ceased to shine forth from Her, and yet Her light grew greater. 5 And She fell to Her knees. And the surface of the waters became turbulent, and the great waves curled over Her, and their white foam could not be seen in all that darkness.

6 And when the waters became calm again, the Mistress of All Things rose to Her feet. 7 For She had conceived a Daughter that was not separate from Her, but one with Her, and the child of Her Light.

CHAPTER II

And She walked across the seas and deep into the forests of the earth until She came upon the deep cave that was at the centre. 2 And She entered the cave. and a star rose above the sacred grove that lay about the cave, brighter and more resplendent than all the stars of the heavens. 3 And the star was seen all over the earth; and the children of the earth were filled with wonder, and they came to the place where the star stood in the sky. 4 And those that were princesses among them brought their crowns to the sacred grove as gifts, and shepherdesses brought the new-dropped lambs, and all the daughters of the earth brought forth the fruits thereof to lay before the cave.

5 But before the cave stood a Genia of the Goddess, robed in a garment so white that the eyes of the earth's children were dazzled, and with a countenance of such great beauty that it was a fearful thing to look upon it. 6 And the daughters of the earth covered their eyes and threw themselves to the ground.

7 And the voice of the Genia was like to the rushing of a thousand waters. 8 And she spoke, saying: Be not afraid, for a new light is dawning over the world. Be not afraid, but approach no further, for if you cannot look on me, how should you look upon my Lady, whose handmaiden I am?

9 And her voice grew gentle, like the wind among the icicles, and sweet beyond all telling. 10 And she spoke, saying: This night shall a Child be born that shall be the Daughter of Light and the Princess of all the World. 11 A Child is coming that shall carry the light of the Goddess into every part of creation; even to the most desolate of the places of darkness. 12 Rejoice, poor wanderers of the earth and exiles from the house of your Mother, for to you shall come a guide and a deliverer.

13 And when the voice of the Genia ceased, a silence fell that was the first true silence since the beginning of the world, and the last that shall be until it end. 14 And the children of the earth watched the sky as the first rays of dawn crept across the heavens.

15 And a cry issued out of the cave, saying: The holy Child is born from the most holy Mother; Light has come forth from Light, Perfection from Perfection.

16 And at once the air was filled with the daughters of heaven, and the sky was ablaze with the radiance of their joy. 17 And they sang aloud to the glory of the Goddess.

18 And when the Shining Ones ceased from their song, the world became quiet again. and the star grew brighter and ever brighter, until it shone more bright than the radiance of all the host of Heaven; and yet so gentle was its light that the eyes of earth's children were

not dazzled. 19 And the colour of the light was not one of the seven, but a wondrous luminance not known within the boundaries of the world.

20 And the Genia at the cave's mouth called forth the children of the earth that they might present their gifts. And the three great princesses of the earth came forward: 21 First the greatest of them, who ruled more land than either of the others and also possessed more treasure. 22 And her crown was of pure gold; and as she took it from her head, the light of the star fell upon it, and it shone with a glister more lovely than any earthly jewel. 23 And she laid it at the feet of the Genia.

24 And the Genia said: It is good that you bring your crown, for you are a great princess, but the Holy Child shall be Princess of all the world.

25 The second princess held neither so much land nor treasure, but she was a maid of deep wisdom and meditation profound. And her crown was of pure silver; and as she took it from her head, the light of the star fell upon it, and it shone with a radiance yet more lovely than that of the golden crown. 26 And she laid it at the feet of the Genia.

27 And the Genia said: It is good that you bring your crown, for you have great wisdom, but the Holy Child is the Daughter of Wisdom Herself.

28 The last princess possessed but few of the world's things, but she was a priestess of the Goddess, and she praised Her in the morning and at evening and at all the seven hours of the day. And her crown was made from glittering crystal; and as she took it from her head the light of the star fell upon it, and she was bathed in rays of a thousand different hues, and the children of the earth drew in their breath at the sight of its beauty. 29 And she laid it at the feet of the Genia.

30 And the Genia said: It is good that you bring your crown, for you are a true and loving priestess and a servant of your people, but the Holy Child shall be Priestess of all the world, and shall serve Her children even to the last and greatest service.

31 And when the Genia ceased to speak, a new voice filled the air, more beautiful and more terrible than hers. And it said:

> Her Name shall be called Inanna,
> For She shall be Lady of Heaven.

32 And the star vanished from the sky, and yet its light remained. and the shape of the light became a vision. 33 And the vision was a vision of the Mistress of All Things, bearing in Her arms the Holy Child. 34 And for all the wondrous things the children of the earth had seen that night, not the whole of them was one thousandth part as wondrous as this vision.

35 And for twelve nights the star returned to the sky; and on the thirteenth night it did not return. And this was a sign of things that were to come.

CHAPTER III

When the Holy Child had grown to the full stature of maidenhood, the Mother of All Things took Her to a high place upon the earth, saying: To You I give the governance of all these things. 2 You shall command the movements of the waters, and the wind shall be Your servant. 3 The seasons of the earth shall You control, and all the times and seasons in the lives of My creatures. 4 Every soul on earth and in the heavens shall be given into Your care, and the highest stars of the firmament shall know You as their Sovereign. 5 For all these things must I put from Me; for they can no longer look upon My brightness.

6 And the Maid ruled over all the world, making the earth grow fruitful and attending to the prayers of Her creatures, and oftentimes making prayers of Her own that they might come closer to the Mother. 7 And Divine Light shone once more upon the earth, and the Maid was a friend to every creature, and all who turned to Her were filled with life, and with the peace that comes of wholeness.

8 For the waxing and waning of twelve moons reigned the Maid. 9 And after the twelfth moon had appeared in the sky, the Mother of All Things called Her Daughter to Her, and spoke to Her, saying: You have

made the whole earth fruitful and brought My light to all the world, have You not satisfaction in Your work?

10 And the Maid replied, saying: I have brought Your light to many places, and yet a place there is which remains ever in darkness; a place beneath all places, in which there is no light. 11 And the ways of entrance to that place are many, for there is a place at the bottom of each earthly soul into which Your light cannot shine.

12 And the Mother asked Her: Do You know what thing it is that You must do if You will bring My light into every place?

13 And the Maid replied: I know what it is that I must do.

14 For She knew that She must descend into the nether regions, giving up the Divine light and going down into that place wherein is no light, but only the profoundest darkness. 15 And this was Her taking on of fate upon Herself.

16 And the Mother of All Things removed the Divine light from Her Daughter, and blessing Her, sent Her forth, saying: Go hence from here, beloved Daughter, for You may no longer look upon Me.

17 And the Children of Heaven led Her forth, and praised Her in strange and gentle songs. 18 And the Maid set Herself apart to pray, and She prayed alone by

the running streams and beneath the full moon, until a new light was kindled within Her, which was the pure light of Her own divinity. 19 Yet while the divine light of Her Mother was undying, the light of the Maid trembled before the winds of death.

20 And the daughters of Heaven delighted in Her gentle light, saying: This trembling light is the glory of all the heavens and more glorious than all the luminaries thereof.

21 And the Maid answered them, saying: I shall carry this light into every place that is, even unto the nethermost regions and the regions of death.

22 And they led Her forth and clothed Her in the white robe of the sacrifice.

CHAPTER IV

The Maid took up the great Moon-Axe, whose silver blades were as the crescents of the moon, in symbol of Her light, and went alone into a desert place. 2 And, knowing that She had not the light of Her Mother upon Her, malefic keres gathered about and beset Her: keres of fear and of dread isolation, and every sort of restriction. 3 And they tore Her soul with their talons, crying: Hope is dead, for the light of the Mother is fallen from You. 4 You shall go down to suffering and death and none shall save You. In the illimitable emptiness of the universe shall You stand alone and none shall give you comfort. 5 In the darkness of eternal night shall You kneel to weep and no hand shall be put upon Your shoulder, but every hand shall be raised against You to do you hurt.

6 And the Maid was filled with trembling, but She answered: Go your ways, for what I have said, that shall I do.

7 And the keres spoke, saying: Be You led by us, and You shall have protection and all good things. 8 The whole of the world shall be Your fortress, and You shall have wealth and magnificence that all the children of the earth shall love You.

9 But the Maid answered: How shall you give to Me that which is Mine? 10 For I am the Princess of the world, and all the children of the earth have been given into My care by he hand of the eternal.

11 Then the keres said: The light of the Eternal is taken from You, and whether these things are or are not Yours, it is we that have the power of them, and we that You must obey if You will be saved.

12 But the Maid replied, saying: That which is right in the deepest heart of things, and in the centre of all being, that is right and none other; and the Truth alone is true. 13 Nor shall all the powers of the earth count against it, neither all the powers of the seas and the skies move it by the smallest fraction in all its vastness. 14 I shall obey none but My Mother, though all your power be turned in fury upon Me.

15 And the keres cried: Not our power, but the power of one far greater from whom our power derives.

16 And the Maid said: Thus may it be.

17 And the keres questioned Her, saying: think You that Your Mother will save You?

18 And the maid answered: She will do what She will do, and blessed is Her Name.

19 And the keres laughed, saying: Then are You abandoned to the uttermost darkness.

20 And the heart of the Maid fainted within Her.

21 And She said: Thus may it be.

CHAPTER V

And the Maid journeyed down into the darkest regions until She came to the great gates of the Nether World. 2 And the gatekeeper cried: Who is it that comes of her own free step upon the realm of the Dark Queen? 3 And the Maid replied: I am the Daughter of She Who is Mother of all.

4 And the gatekeeper said: Give me your axe, and You may pass. And the Maid gave the great Moon-Axe into her hands, and the vast oaken gate swung open that She might pass through.

5 And the Maid came to a second gate, and was again halted by the keeper thereof. And the gatekeeper said: Give me the circlet from Your head, and You may pass. 6 And the Maid gave the silver circlet into her hands and passed through the gate.

7 And She came to a third gate, and the gatekeeper said: Give me Your white linen head dress and You may pass. And She did this and passed bareheaded through the gate.

8 And She came to a fourth gate, and the gatekeeper said: Give me Your blue cloak and You may pass. And She gave Her blue cloak into the hands of the gatekeeper, and passed through the gate.

9 And She came to a fifth gate, and the gatekeeper said: Give me your sandals and You may pass. And She unlaced Her sandals and passed barefooted through the gate.

10 And She came to a sixth gate, and the gatekeeper said: Give me the silver girdle about Your waist and You may pass. And She unbound Her silver girdle and passed through the gate wearing only Her white robe.

11 And She came to a seventh gate, and the gatekeeper said: Give me Your hair and You may pass. And She bowed Her head, and Her hair was shorn from Her, and She passed into the chamber of the Dark Queen.

12 And the Dark Queen spoke, saying: Are You the Princess of the world, and the Daughter of She Who is Mother of all? And the Maid replied: I am She.

13 And Her hands were bound, and the daughters of the Dark Queen taunted Her and beat Her, and pulled Her short hair. And She was dragged to Her knees before the Dark Queen.

14 And the Dark Queen rose to her feet, and so terrible was her aspect that her daughters fled to the furthest part of the chamber. 15 And she turned her eyes upon the Maid, that have been beheld by no creature of

the upper world. For her eyes are the eyes of death. 16 And the Maid looking upon her eyes, became a lifeless corse and a dead thing upon the ground.

17 And at the centre of the Nether World there stood a great pillar, reaching to the roof of that world. 18 And the daughters of the Dark Queen took the corse of the Maid, and hung it high upon that pillar. 19 And above Her head they hung the great Moon-Axe, in symbol of the greatness of the deed.

CHAPTER VI

Now from the time when the Daughter of Heaven had passed through the first gate of Hell, a barrenness had fallen on the earth; and neither bird had sung nor any flower showed its beauty forth; nor was there joy in any heart. 2 But when the Maid was slain upon the pillar of the world, an awful darkness fell on all the earth. 3 And the rivers of the earth ceased to flow, but drained away into the salt sea, and the sea ceased to move, but stood still in awful stagnancy. 4 And there was drouth in all the earth. And neither maid bore child nor ewe brought forth the lamb. And every growing thing began to wither from its roots. 5 And in the nights were neither moon nor stars, and the heat of the sun by day was terrible.

6 And the Mother of All Things wept and walked in sorrow over earth and Heaven.

7 And the children of the earth prayed to Her, weeping for the world and for Her Daughter. 8 And in the darkness after the second day, a silver star appeared in the heavens, whose brightness was too great for them to look upon.

9 And the children of earth rejoiced saying: It is the Mistress of All Things, come to seek Her Daughter.

And the Dark Queen ordered the gates of Hell to be shut and barred against Her.

10 And the gatekeeper stood within the gate, and cried: Who is it that comes upon the realm of the Dark Queen? And She answered, saying: I am the Mistress of all that is, and the Mother of My Daughter. 12 Give Me entrance, for if you give Me not entrance, I will smash the bolt and shatter the gatepost. I will raise up the great gate of Hell and break it asunder.

13 But the gatekeeper opened not the gate. And the Mistress of All Things clapped Her hands together, so that the whole world shook, and the great gate of Hell was shattered in fragments, and the nether regions trembled to the very foundations. 14 And the gatekeeper covered her eyes and fled, for she could not look upon the brightness of the Mistress of All Things.

15 And the Mistress of All Things came into the Nether World; and the six gatekeepers flung wide their gates and fled.

16 And Her Geniae took down the corse of Her Daughter, and laid it upon Her knees; and She wept anew, for none but She could know the awful depth of the oblivion in which Her Daughter lay. And She sprinkled on the corse the water of Life, which She had gathered from the holy tears of Her Own sorrow. 17 And Her Daughter rose again and was alive again. 18 And amid tears of joy, They embraced and were one.

And after this the Daughter stood alone. 19 And the souls of the Nether World were awakened by Her gentle light, and followed Her through the shattered gates of Hell.

20 And when they beheld Her, the children of the earth rejoiced, and the rivers flowed again, and the sea began to move.

21 And the children of the earth cried: Lift up your voices in song and laughter, for the Princess of the World was dead and is alive again, was broken and is whole; and there is no place whereto Her joyous rule does not extend. 22 Give praise to the Mother of All Things and praise Her Daughter

23 Rejoice, for the world is renewed.

CHAPTER VII

And as She walked, the children of the earth threw blossoms before Her, and though Her feet rested on them, yet they were not bruised. 2 And She reigned over all the earth, bringing all nature back to life, and all life back to the true law and rhythm of nature. And the whole world knew Her as its Princess. 3 And the children of earth were filled with love for Her, and gathered about Her with tears of joy, touching Her robes and giving themselves to Her in their hearts. 4 And She gathered them together and taught them many things, saying: You have gained knowledge of the world, but I say, be not wise with the wisdom of the world, nor proud with the pride of the world, nor strait with the dignity of the world, neither lose your self in any of the ways and fashions of the world, but come to Me as little children in the pure simplicity of your hearts and the virgin innocence of your souls – for truly, all of you are children in the eyes of your Mother, and I shall receive all who come as Her children. Come you so to Me and all faults shall be forgiven. And She showed them how to offer Sacrifice to the Mother of All Things. 5 And She said: When the time is come for Me to go from you, still I shall be with you; and shall never leave you, not for one fragment of an hour until we are together in completion. 6 But I shall unite you all who love Me in one great body; 7 The highest and the lowest, the living and the dead, those who falter at the door, and those who have climbed to the highest tower, all shall be one in My body which I have given to the world, and all shall be nourished by My Spirit.

8 And they understood Her not, but only wept that She must leave them. And She spoke no more of this, but taught them, and revealed many hidden things, such as might fill an hundred books.

9 And when the time was at hand, two Geniae descended, one on either side of Her, and She went with them into Heaven.

10 And the children of Heaven greeted Her, crying: Hail, Princess of the World; Hail, Queen of Heaven. And they placed a crown of stars about Her head. 11 And the blue night was Her cloak, and the stars of the sky the crown about Her head, and the moon lay at Her feet. And they cried again: Hail, Queen of Heaven.

12 And thus began Her dear and glorious reign. And for the children of Heaven, Her very Presence was the completion of their joy. 13 And She poured forth Her grace and blessing from Her hands upon them and upon the earth. And Her grace and blessing were as rays of perfect Light which penetrate the heart and flood the soul.

14 And She said to them: Do not forget your sisters on the earth, but move yourselves among them

and hear their voices; lend them succour and breathe with them in their upward aspiration. 15 And when a soul in true devotion passes from the earth, lead her to the portal of Heaven and the garden of Avala, and give her rest, and provision her with treasures of the Spirit to help her on her way.

16 And She entered the great Temple of Heaven, where the spirits of earth's children were gathered at the Sacrifice, even as their souls were gathered on earth.

17 And She stood at the great Altar and took up a wheaten loaf, and spoke, saying: 18 Like to the corn, My body was cut down by the scythe of death; and like to the corn did it rise anew. 19 For I am the ear of corn that is reaped in silence.

20 And She said: Like to the grain was my body broken between the stones of death. And saying thus, she broke the bread between Her hands.

21 And She gave the fragments of the bread to the spirits of earth's children, saying: Here is my body that is broken for you. Eat My body, that you may be one with My body, and may be one body in Me.

22 And She poured out Her Spirit from Her hands into a great Chalice, and Her Spirit lay as wine within the Chalice. 23 And She said: Even as you have offered Me bread in Sacrifice, so I give you the bread of My body; and as you have poured out libations of wine to

Me, so I pour out the eternal libation of My eternal Spirit.

24 And as it is performed above in the spirit, so is it reflected below in the body and the soul, and through the reflection do earth's children have part in the Real. 25 And so were the things that are told in this book reflected in the hearts of maids, that all might read them and draw closer to She that acted them.

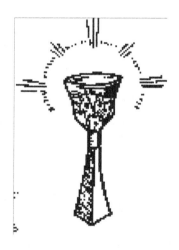

Our Lady is exalted among the daughters
    of Heaven.
Shining Inanna, Star of the Sea,
Robed in celestial light.
She abases the cruel and the proud,
And hearkens to the plea of the lowly.
The rich who deny Her godhead find not
    contentment,
But blessed is the humblest of Her
    servants.
She delivers the captive into Her care,
And takes the hand of the fallen.
May the whole world praise Thee, beloved
    Inanna,
May Thy glory be told of in all the
    earth.
Let then exalt Thy dominion
And Thy valiant courage
And glorify Thy holy Name.
Have mercy on Thy servant who gives Thee
    blessing
And take her hand in need and suffering.
In illness and distress give her the
    gift of life.
May she go forever in joy and delight
To magnify Thy holy Name

Before all the peoples of the world.

The earliest surviving
version of this prayer
is about 4,000 years
old

THE CATECHISM

OF THE CHILDREN OF

THE GODDESS

ISSUED UNDER THE HAND OF THE GODDESS BY

Lux Madriana

THE

CATECHISM

OF THE

CHILDREN

OF THE

GODDESS

CONTENTS

ooooOOOoooo

Note

The Use of the Catechism

The Catechism contains the essential tenets of catholic Madrianism, and should be fully known by all candidates for Initiation. Learning the Catechism should be undertaken in a devotional spirit as part of the inner preparation for Initiation, and not merely as an academic exercise. Passages set in brackets need not be learned by the initiand.

I

THE ORIGIN OF

THE SOUL

1.   From whence do you come and where is your first origin?

+   I was created from before the beginning of time by the Goddess out of the overflowing of Her divine love.

2.   What manner of creature are you?

+   I am the reflection of a fragment of Her eternal Spirit.

3.   What have been your actions since the beginning of time?

+   I have passed through many states of existence and many forms of life (although I can remember but a little).

4.   How came you upon this wheel of countless existences?

+   In the beginning, my soul turned from the love of the Goddess and so fell into exile from her natural state.

5.   What is the natural state of your soul?

+   The natural state of my soul is Perfect Union with the Goddess, which is the state of pure delight.

II

DEITY

The Trinity

6.   What is the first cause of existence?

+   The Goddess is the first cause of existence, for She created the manifest universe.

7.   What is the Goddess?

+   The Goddess is the one Spirit of the universe, complete in Herself, uncreated and infinite in potency, perception and perfection.

8.   What is the Mystery of the Divine Trinity?

+   That there is only one Goddess, yet She is three Persons.

9.   What is a Mystery?

+   A Mystery is a truth beyond the grasp of reason which the Goddess has non-theless revealed to us.

10.   Who are the three Persons of the Trinity?

+   Our Celestial Mother, Her Divine Daughter and the Dark Mother who is Absolute Deity.

11.   Who is our Celestial Mother?

+   The Mother is the Creator of the world and the Ground of all being.

12.   What is Her Nature?

+   She is pure Life, pure Light and pure energy.

13.   What are Her acts?

+   All life, all action and all thought flow from Her.

14.   Who is Her Daughter?

+   Her Daughter is Princess of the World, Priestess of the World and Queen of Heaven.

15.   What is Her Nature?

+   She is pure love.

16.   What are Her Acts?

+   As Princess of the World, She governs all the cycles of life and nature; as Priestess of the World, She gives us Communion with Her Mother; as Queen of Heaven, she shall bring us at last to the Celestial Throne.

17.   Who is the Dark Mother?

+   She is Absolute Deity, Who existed before the beginning of existence and is beyond being and unbeing.

18.   What is Her Nature?

+   She is outside space and time; She is all that is and all that is not.

19.   What are Her Acts?

+   The exhalation of Her breath or Spirit is our Mother, the Creator of the world. Of Her other Acts, our minds cannot conceive.

20.   Does Trinity last only for the period of manifest creation?

+   No, Trinity is the eternal Nature of Deity.

The Nature of Deity

21.   Had the Goddess any beginning?

+   The Goddess had no beginning and will have no end.

22.   When did the Goddess create the world?

+   She creates it now and in every moment; if She ceased to create it, it would cease to exist.

23.   Where is the Goddess?

+   She is in every place at all times.

24.   What is the name of the Goddess?

+   She has been given many names by many different peoples.

25.   Yet are there many Goddesses?

+   No, there is only one Goddess.

26.   Are there any other Deities?

+   There are no other Deities.

27.   Who are those others that some worship as Deities?

+   Some are Geniae and creatures of the higher spheres; others are keres or mere creatures of illusion. (see *Note*)

28.   Could the Goddess have a special relationship with one or more of these higher creatures?

+   She could have no special relationship.

29.   What is the reason of this?

+   Firstly, She alone is uncreated; all other beings are of Her creation, therefore none can exist on Her own level.
        Secondly, the highest relationship between creature and Deity is that of Perfect Union; this is the final aim of *every* soul, and no special relationship can be higher than this.

30.   What are the powers of the Goddess?

+   The powers of the Goddess are infinite; no thing is impossible to Her.

31.   What is the knowledge of the Goddess?

+   The knowledge of the Goddess is infinite; she knows all that is, all that has been and all that is to come.

III

GOOD AND EVIL

32.   What is a moral decision?

+   A moral decision is a decision between good and evil.

33.   What is Absolute Good?

+   The Goddess is Absolute Good.

34.   What is relative good?

+   Relative good is a state of moving closer to the Goddess.

35.   What is relative evil?

+   Relative evil is a state of moving further from the Goddess.

36.   What is absolute evil?

+   Absolute evil is the complete absence of the Goddess.

37.   Can absolute evil exist?

+   Absolute evil cannot exist, for the Goddess is the essence of existence; therefore a thing completely without Her would have no existence.

38.   What is the highest good of all creatures?

+   The highest good of all creatures is Perfect Union with the Goddess.

39.   When we speak of moving closer to the Goddess, do we speak of the material plane or of the spiritual plane?

+   Of the spiritual plane.

40.   What do you mean by moving closer to the Goddess on the spiritual plane?

+   I mean that I become more like my true self and more in harmony with Her.

41.   What do you mean by moving further from the Goddess on the spiritual plane?

+   I mean that I become more unlike my true self and more out of harmony with her.

42.   What is your true self?

My true self is the perfect expression of a facet of Deity.

43.   What is the general nature of your true self?

+   My true self is a creature of infinite beauty, existing in a state of perfect happiness and complete harmony with the Goddess, and subject to no limitation of any kind.

44.   What is the particular nature of your true self?

+   Every facet of Deity is utterly unique; so also are the creatures which express them.

Imperfect Existence: matter and limitation

45.   What was your first moral action?

+   My first moral action was to turn from the Goddess at the beginning of time.

46.   Was this act good or evil?

+   It was the primal act of evil.

47.   Did you alone perform this act?

+   Many creatures performed it.

48.   What was the nature of things before this act?

+   Before this act all things were Perfect Forms or Divine Ideas.

49.   What was the nature of things after this act?

+   After this act all things became matter that they might have existence apart form the Goddess.

50.   What is matter?

+   All things below the level of pure spirit are material.

51.   Is matter purely physical?

+   No, matter is both physical and non-physical.

52.   Is matter evil?

+   Insofar as matter reflects Divine Ideas it is good; insofar as it is but a broken and imperfect reflection of them, it is evil.

53.   What are the three chief parts of material or non-spiritual existence which affect us in this world?

+   The physical, the emotional and the mental.

54.   What is the characteristic of imperfect existence which is absent from perfect existence?

+   Limitation.

55.   What is limitation?

+   Limitation is the inability of the soul to accomplish her will (on the lowest planes it is manifest as the scarcity of material resources); it is the source of suffering and of all other evils.

56.   What is the source of the evil of limitation?

+   Separation from the Goddess is the source of limitation, for the Goddess is unlimited and so also are all souls in harmony with Her.

The Foundations of Good Action

57.   Since your first moral act, have you committed others?

+   Almost every act committed since that time has had a moral character.

58.   What is the moral character of a material act?

+ It is its spiritual quality of good or evil.

59. How is that determined?

+ It is determined by whether the act is in accordance with the three Primary Virtues.

60. What are the three Primary Virtues?

+ They are Life, or Wholeness; Light, or Energy; and Love, or Harmony.

61. Where do we learn of these virtues?

+ In the book called the ***Crystal Tablet***.

62. What are the five Rules of Life by which we may achieve these virtues?

+ They are:
    1. To love the Goddess.
    2. To love all Her creatures.
    3. To love my true self.
    4. To seek to make my every act a perfect gift to Her, and to offer to her all my happiness and all my suffering.
    5. To seek to bring all souls closer to Her.

IV

THE QUEST OF THE SOUL

63.   Have you lived before this life?

+   I have lived before.

64.   How long have you lived?

+   I have lived since the beginning of time.

65.   Of this, how much can you remember?

+   I can remember only a little.

66.   How long shall you live?

+   I shall live forever.

67.   What will happen when you die?

+   If I have lived as a good Madrian, I shall go after death into the paradise of the Daughter, called Avala, to rest in happiness.

68.   Shall you then inhabit a body?

+   No, I shall be all soul.

69.   What is soul?

+   Soul is the spiritual creature which is the real '*I*'.

70.   Are souls both female and male?

+   No, all spiritual creatures are female, for maleness is a thing of the material world.

71.   Do male creatures have souls?

+   Yes, male creatures have female souls.

72.   Shall all creatures become pure soul after death?

+   No, those who in life have rejected the spiritual shall retain strong emotional and mental materiality.

73.   Shall they keep their material bodies?

+   No, and having lost them, they shall flounder in darkness and confusion.

74.   Shall this state last forever?

+   No, eventually they shall continue on their journey; either further from the Mother, or else turning again to Her.

75.   Shall any soul be lost forever?

+   No, in the fullness of time, every soul shall realise the full horror of evil and shall turn to the Good.

76.   Shall you remain forever in Avala?

+   No eventually I shall continue my journey toward the Mother.

77.   Can your soul approach directly to the Mother?

+   She cannot.

78.   Why is this?

+   Because, having turned form Her at the beginning of time, I am not absolutely good. Therefore my soul cannot exist in Her presence.

79.   In what way, then, can you approach Deity?

+   I can approach Her daughter.

80.   How is this so?

+   Because, seeing the plight of humanity, she severed Herself from Her Mother in order that we may come to Her.

81.   By what means did She do this?

+   By Her descent into the under world and Her Death.

82.   Did She rise from that death?

+   Yes, and as She rose, so shall we rise, that we may come to the Mother.

83.   And shall the Daughter guide you on your way from Avala?

+   She is always guiding the soul that turns to Her.

V

EKKLESIA MADRIANA

The Ekklesia of Our Lady

84.   What is Ekklesia?

+   Ekklesia is the body of all souls who are in communion with the Goddess.

85.   Is Ekklesia of this world only?

+   No, Ekklesia exists on every plane of being.

86.   Does Ekklesia include only human souls?

+   No, Ekklesia includes heras, Geniae and other souls, both incarnate and discarnate.

87.   What are the three ways by which a human soul may enter Ekklesia?

+   By Charisma, by Initiation and by Offering.

88.   What is Charismatic entry?

+ Charismatic entry occurs when a soul, through her devotion, is received by the Goddess without any earthly Sacrament.

89. What is Initiation?

+ Initiation is the Sacrament by which Ekklesia receives a mature person.

90. What takes place at this Sacrament?

+ The initiate dies to the world of matter and is reborn into Ekklesia.

91. What is Offering?

+ Offering is the ritual by which an infant is offered to the Goddess and is received into Ekklesia.

92. Is Offering sufficient for a whole lifetime?

+ No, the child should later receive her own Initiation.

93. What is the reason for Offering?

+ It allows the child to enjoy the spiritual benefits of being a member of Ekklesia, helps her to draw closer to the Goddess, and makes her a member of Her earthly family from the beginning.

94.   What is a Sacrament?

+   A Sacrament is an act which takes place at once on earth and in the Pleroma.

95.   What is the Pleroma?

+   The Pleroma is the realm of pure Being where alone an action can attain complete reality.

96.   What is Communion?

+   Communion is the Sacrament through which initiates of Ekklesia nourish their souls by union with the Goddess.

97.   How often should a Madrian initiate take Communion?

+   If possible, a Madrian initiate should take Communion regularly. she must take Communion at least on each Major Festival unless prevented by extreme difficulty.

98.   Who can celebrate Communion?

+   Only a priestess can celebrate Communion.

99.   What is a priestess?

+ A priestess is a maid chosen by the Goddess to serve Her earthly children.

100. How does a maid become a priestess?

+ Either by Charisma or by Initiation.

101. Is the Initiation of a priestess a Sacrament?

+ The initiation of a priestess is a Sacrament.

102. What are the two duties of a priestess?

+ 1. To transmit the Power of the Goddess through the Sacraments and other rituals.
2. To have care of the souls of Her children in devotional and other matters.

103. What is the Sacrifice?

+ The Sacrifice is an act of devotion to the Goddess.

104. Is the Sacrifice a Sacrament?

+ The Sacrifice is not a Sacrament.

105. How often must a Madrian initiate make Sacrifice?

+   A Madrian initiate must make Sacrifice or take Communion at least on every natural Rite unless prevented by extreme difficulty.

The Cult Domestic

106.   What is the Cult Domestic?

+   The Cult Domestic is the whole religious life of a Madrian household centring upon a regular domestic Sacrifice.

107.   Who shall celebrate the Sacrifice?

+   The spiritual head of the household shall celebrate the Sacrifice.

108.   Who is the spiritual head of the household?

+   Either the mother, or else the temporal matriarch, or any other maid who has made a solemn undertaking to act as spiritual head of her household.

109.   Who shall celebrate if she is absent?

+   Either her eldest daughter, or any other maid whom she has chosen to act as her surrogate.

110.   What is a Madrian household?

+ A Madrian household is any group of Madrians who live together and all who are dear to them.

111. Should the Cult Domestic replace the Communion of Ekklesia?

+ The Cult Domestic should never replace the Communion of Ekklesia unless there is no practising priestess in the area.

Personal Devotion

112. How shall you preserve the spiritual health of your soul?

+ By rejecting the false materialistic values of the world, and seeking to live in gentleness, generosity and innocence.

113. How should you emend the faults of your soul?

+ By penitence and true devotion.

114. What is prayer?

+ Prayer is a personal communion with the Goddess.

115.   What is the importance of prayer?

+   Prayer is the breath of my spiritual life.

116.   When should you pray?

+   I should pray frequently, but at least each morning and each night.

117.   What is morning prayer?

+   Morning prayer is an offering of the day's events to the Goddess, and an asking of Her blessing upon them.

118.   What is night prayer?

+   Night prayer is a return to full contemplation of the Goddess at the end of the day.

119.   Should prayer be a mere repeating of words?

+   No, prayer should be a bringing of my whole being to the Goddess.

120.   What are the other chief forms of personal devotion?

+   Meditation upon the Goddess and Her Mysteries, and saying the Rosary.

121.   How should you end your devotions?

+   By saying the Silver Star and making the Pentacle upon myself.

Note

The words "Deity" and "Goddess" are used throughout this book in their full sense of "the one Creator of the universe". It follows, then, that there can be no other. We may, of course, honour the Goddess under many names, and honour all the Geniae of different offices – such as Hestia, Genia of the home, or Pallas, Genia of wisdom; or of places – the tutelary Geniae of nations or of temples; Our Lady of particular shrines and sacred places.

It is often hard to know whether we honour a higher spirit or an aspect of our Lady; but the distinction is not greatly important, for every soul expresses a facet of the resplendent jewel of Deity, and the more advanced the soul, the more completely is she an expression of our Lady.

Thus we may freely speak of the Goddess Athene or the Goddess Hestia without losing the fundamental truth that deity is One.

ooooOOOoooo

The term "maid", as used in this book, refers to any woman who has completed the fourteenth year of her present incarnation.

Appendix 1: MAKING THE PENTACLE

The Pentacle is a powerful protective symbol. It is a variant of the five-pointed star of the Goddess (the Madrian Rosary, the archetype of the rosaries used in all the masculist world religions, has one decade for each point of the Pentacle, or for each petal of the Rose – hence its name). To form the Pentacle, one should first touch the forehead, then, visualising a line of silver etheric light, bring the hand diagonally to touch the left hip, then draw another line to touch the right shoulder; then the left shoulder; the right hip and finally the forehead again.

One of the most important symbolisms of the Pentacle is that of the elements or seasons. The uppermost point represents the fifth element: Spirit, and the fifth season Moura. The other elements are arranged sunwise (clockwise) around the remaining points in order of the seasons: Water (Spring), Fire (Summer), Earth (Autumn) and Air (Winter). See diagram.

The forming of the Pentacle symbolises the Cosmic Drama. We touch first Spirit, which represents the purity of the first creation; then Earth – the descent into matter; then Water (the Easter element) – the sacrifice of our Lady in coming to us; then Air – the star of Her coming and the bringing of Her Light; she brings us to the consuming Fire of Her Mother's love – to "The Rose that is a Flame and the Flame that is a Rose";

through the Divine Fire, we are purged of imperfection and return to our first purity, touching Spirit again.

As well as its devotional value, the Pentacle can form a barrier against harmful spiritual and psychological influences.

One very effective visualisation, having made the Pentacle, is to envision a small flame at the tip of each point. Allow these to grow in size until their bases meet at the centre of the Pentacle. Thus each is a fiery petal of one great Rose of flame. This is particularly apt for the final decade of the Rosary, when completing the Great Pentacle and contemplating the Mystery of the Rose of the World.

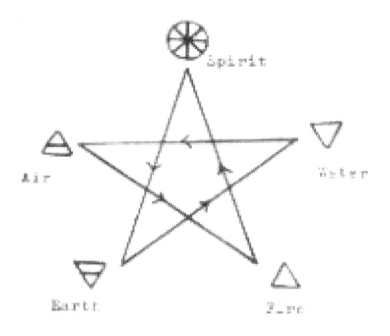

Appendix 2: THE ROSARY

The Rosary is usually a looped string of beads (though it may also be a cord containing knots). The beads are arranged in five decades or groups of ten. There is a single bead at the beginning and end, and one between each decade. The closed loop represents both the walled rose-garden and eternity.

For each bead of the decades we say the Silver Star, and for each single bead we say the Prayer of Eternity.

Begin by composing yourself in quietness, then make the Pentacle upon yourself and say the Rosary Prayer before starting.

Each decade represents a point of the Pentacle. Beginning at Earth and Autumn, we move sunwise, meditating on the Mysteries of each as we pray.

Earth; Autumn; the Golden Apple; the Mystery of Divine Life; our Lady the Mother as Ground of all being.

Air; Winter; the Star; the Mystery of the Nativity.

Spirit; Moura; the Cross (or Labrys); the Mystery of the death of our Lady.

Water; Spring; the Dove; the Mystery of the resurrection of our Lady.

Fire; Summer; the Rose; the Mystery of the Rose of the World; complete personal assumption in the Mother.

Although a child can say the Rosary, a lifetime cannot exhaust its depth. Frequent Rosary devotion will lead the soul ever deeper into the fivefold structure of the Universal Mystery.

In the full Rosary, the process is repeated three times, meditating upon the Mysteries in the Life aspect, the Light aspect and the Love aspect. But this is a rather advanced exercise.

The Rosary is a powerful generator of spiritual energy as well as a purifying force. Each completed Rosary not only confers great spiritual benefit on the individual, but is a real force for good in this world. Regarded as a personal sacrifice, the Rosary is a small but beautiful gift to our Lady. For each Rosary is not only a thing said and a thing done, but a thing created – it is a shining Pentacle of spiritual force.

Appendix 3

The Silver Star

Silver Star of the waters
that have laughed all the world into being,
beyond all knowing
        is the splendour of Your light.
Enfold my spirit in Your mighty hand
that the pure stream of Your force
        may flow within me
in this world
and in all the worlds to come.

A Morning Offering

Celestial Mother, grant me this day that every work I do
shall be as lovingly and well performed as though I were
to give it into Your divine hands.

Fill me with Your energy, that I may both give
beauty to the world and perceive the beautiful in all of
Your creation.

Grant that this day shall add a stone to the temple
of my soul.

An Evening Prayer

Mother, to Whom all the thousands of the days are as one, and yet Who knowest more of the small events of my past day than I; receive my spirit at the ending of the day, and protect her through the night.

Rosary Prayer

Beloved Kyria, Who have suffered in a way I cannot understand that You might come to me, I offer You my hand; lead my soul into the garden of the Rosary, that she may rest among the mystic roses of Your love.

Prayer of Eternity

Eternal is the Light of the Mother,
Eternal is the Love of the Daughter,
Eternal is their completion
        in the wholeness of the Absolute;
And glorious is Eternity.

Daughter of Light

Daughter of Light,
> that reignest as Queen of Heaven,
> all praise and honour we joyfully
>> give to You.
Give us to learn that You are by us
> in every act we make.
Teach us obedience and humility
> and joy of heart
> that comes of self-forgetting.
Help us to be clear mirrors of Your Love;
> reflecting all the beauty of the world;
> for beauty is the echo of Eternity.
Fix our hearts on the Eternal
> and let us not be turned from You by
> transient things.
Rescue us from the hands of darkness
> that we may serve You with all our being
> here and in Your bright Eternity.

A Grace Before Meals

Lady of all nature, we thank You for the gifts of Your creation. Grant us Your blessing now and eternally.

Some Short Prayers

Praised be the Mother; praised be the Daughter; praised be Absolute deity.

Lady, help me to make this act a perfect gift to You.

I am Your child, Mother, now and eternally; let my heart turn from these transient things.
(against the urgings of the false self)

Inanna, let Your dear sacrifice strengthen me.

Kyria, I know that You are with me, have ever been and ever shall be.

A Canticle of the Goddess

There is no thing fairer on the earth
    than She,
Nor any thing upon the Heaven fairer.
Before Her splendour does the noon-day sun
Burn as the dying embers of a fire.
Daughter of Light
Does not Thy Spirit breathe in all
    created things?
Is not all darkness scattered by Thy fire?
And but for Thee would not all cosmos
    decompose?
Would not the black abyss of chaos
    swallow all?
And as Thine universal music reins the
    furthest spheres,
So does it tune the beating of my heart.
For as the running doe longs fort the
    cooling streams,
So is my soul athirst for Thy dear Grace;
And as long hunger brings the limbs to
    weakness,
Trembles my soul for confluence with Thee.
Have pity on my soul and end her trembling,
Fill her with the good nourishment of
    Thy love;
For there is no thing other that will
    cool her fever
And there is no way other she shall find

content.
O, let my soul be chastened by her
      suffering;
O, let her care no longer for her pride;
O, let her cry to You in childlike
      trustfulness;
Let her be humbled in Your gentle light.
Of mine own self can I accomplish nothing;
Only so far as You are acting through me.
How dull my soul is; like the ashes of
      a fire:
But piercèd through with Thine eternal
      rays,
Is she not radiant as the noon-day sun?
There is no thing fairer on the earth
      than Thee,
Nor any thing upon the Heaven fairer.

The Rite of
SACRIFICE

ISSUED UNDER THE HAND OF THE GODDESS BY

Lux Madriana

THE

RITE

OF

SACRIFICE

CONTENTS

"We will do everything
that we have vowed;
offer Sacrifice
to the Queen of Heaven
and pour out libations to Her"

INTRODUCTION
to the Rite

Through the Rite of Sacrifice, we come as close as we can come to full communion with the Goddess without taking the Sacrament of Communion. It is therefore a ritual of profound spiritual meaning and effect. Performed faithfully, it will begin to lead the soul out of the prim little antechamber of mundane consciousness and into the great halls and passageways of the unconscious self, through whose magnificent windows streams the splendid sunlight of our Lady's love.

Since it is not a Sacrament, the celebrant does not have to be a priestess, and the participants need not be initiates. It is preferable that the celebrant should be an initiate, but if no female initiate is present, any non-initiate maid may celebrate.

A handmaid is not necessary to the Rite, but if one is present, she will be responsible for all the practical aspects of preparing the Sacrifice, and will speak all the parts marked C/H. Otherwise they are spoken by the celebrant.

The Cult Domestic

This is a cult of regular Sacrifice within a Madrian household (a household is defined as any group of Madrians who live together and all who are dear to them). It is celebrated by the spiritual head of the household – often the mother, but any maid may undertake to become spiritual head of her household. The Cult is a great asset to Madrian life, although it should not, in the case of initiates, replace regular Communion.

The Times

Rites can be held at any time, but should always be held on natural rite days and Major Festivals, when the appropriate lection texts and prefaces should be used.

The Natural Rites and Lection Texts

+ NEW MOON: **Creation** Chapter 1
+ DAY OF ARTEMIS (5th day after New Moon): **Creation** Chapters 2 and 3
+ FULL MOON: **Creation** Chapter 1
+ HALF MOON DAY (the Monday nearest to being equidistant between Full Moon and New Moon): **Creation** Chapters 2 and 3.

The Major Festivals and Texts

(The passages in brackets should be used as prefaces to the Festival Rites)

+ 1st Columbina; The Resurrection of Our Lady: **Mythos of the Divine Maid** Chapter VI (Chapter VI, verses 21-23).

+ 5th Columbina; The Day of our Sovereign Lady: **Crystal Tablet** 30-52 (**Mythos VII**, 2).

+ 14th Maia; The Exultation of the Queen of Heaven: **Mythos** VII (VII, 10 and 11).

+ First new or full moon after 9th Rosea; The Festival of the Rose of the World: **Creation** 1 and **C.T.** 18-29 (**C.T.** 49-50).

+ 22nd Kerea; The Festival of Regeneration: **C.T.** 1-17 (**C.T.** 13-14)

+ 17th Mala; The Feast of Divine Life: **C.T.** 12-29 (**C.T.** 12).

+ 1st Samhain; Samhain, The Feast of the Dead: **C.T.**1-11 and 18-29 (**Mythos** VI, 19).

+ 23rd Samhain; The Festival of Artemis: **Mythos** VII (VII, 6 and 7).

+ First new or full moon after 1st Astraea; the commencement of the Advent: The natural rite text and **Mythos** I shall be read at all natural rites during the Advent, and the Preface shall be the words of the Genia from **Mythos** II, 10-12.

+ First new or full moon after 24 th Astraea, unless this should fall before the end of the month, in which case, the first natural rite thereafter; The Nativity of Our Lady: **Mythos** I and II (II, 15).

+ 10th Brighde; The Feast of Lights: **Mythos** III (II, 30).

+ 28th Brighde; Eve of Moura: **Mythos** III and IV (**Mythos** II, 30). **Mythos** IV shall be read at all Rites during Moura.

+ Hiatus: **Mythos** V and VI, 1-6 (no Preface).

The Sacred and Profane Months

Columbina	(Mar 21 – Apr 17)
Maia	(Apr 18 – May 15)
Hera	(May 16 – Jun 12)
Rosea	(Jun 13 – Jul 10)
Kerea	(Jul 11 – Aug 7)
Hesperis	(Aug 8 – Sep 4)
Mala	(Sep 5 – Oct 2)
Hathor	(Oct 3 – Oct 30)

Samhain	(Oct 31 – Nov 27)
Astraea	(Nov 28 – Dec 25)
Hestia	(Dec 26 – Jan 22)
Brighde	(Jan 23 – Feb 19)
Moura	(Feb 20 – Mar 19)

The Hiatus corresponds to Mar 20 except on leap years when it is two days corresponding to Mar 19 and 20. In these years 11th Moura and not 10th corresponds to 1 Mar, and the secular calendar runs one day behind the normal correspondences until 1st Columbina.

The Altar

Any table may be used. It should be covered by a violet cloth which is used for no other purpose. Alternatively, the cloth may correspond to the seasonal colour for Communion. It should have a statue of our Lady, the Sacrifice, a Chalice containing wine, a brazier and incense. It may also have flowers and candles.

The Sacrifice

Usually a small honey-cake made by one who is present at the Sacrifice.

The Brazier

Usually a bowl containing a low candle, over which a wire frame on which the Sacrifice may be placed, or a bowl containing charcoal of the kind used for incense.

Incense

Usually Rose (for the Mother) or Frankincense (for the Daughter). For the Mother one may also use Red Sandalwood, Ambergris, Musk, Benzoin, Verbena, Vanillin, Myrtle, Patchouli or Calamus. For the Maid, one may also use White Sandalwood, Camphor, Copal, Jasmine, Eucalyptus, Menthol or Rosemary. Either type of Sandalwood, or any combination of Mother and Maid incenses may be used as an incense of Mother-and-Child. Incense may be used in cone, stick or crystal form.

The Chalice

This may be any suitable container with a stem and a base (the simplest form is a wine glass) which should be set aside for the purpose.

The Amphora

This is a container for the remains of the sacrifice. If it is of an appropriate and pleasing design and material it may take its place on the Altar. The remains of the Sacrifice should be returned to nature, being consigned to the sea or to a river or buried in the earth.

The Place

Should be lighted by candles. The Altar should face west so that all except the celebrant face east.

The Pentacle

The celebrant should trace the Pentacle on the air with her right hand, beginning with the line from the uppermost point to the lower left hand point. To make the pentacle on yourself, touch with your right hand in order; forehead, left hip, right shoulder, left shoulder, right hip and forehead again.

The Name of Power

Is pronounced yot-hay-voe, but the aspirate is more like an audible breathing than the usual English 'H'.

Regularity and Perfection

The two most important instructions for the Rite are: perform it regularly and perform it perfectly. Regularity is necessary because the Rite is not just an act; it is a continuous Cult which has been carried on since the beginning of earthly existence and perhaps before. It is a bond of love and honour between the human soul and the Divine. When you undertake the Rite of Sacrifice, you are saying "Mother, I want to take on this obligation for Your sake; I want to carry the torch of Your ancient Rite all the days of my life, and if sometimes it becomes a burden to me, grant me grace that I shall not let it fall. Let me suffer that small burden joyously in Your dear Name". If you cannot say that, then it is better not to perform the Rite of Sacrifice; but if you fear that circumstances may prevent you from making regular Sacrifice, do not hesitate, for our Lady never asks more of any soul than she is able to perform.

Perfection is partly practical; the celebrant should aim at perfection of word and act. It is best that she should know the words of the Rite, but at least she should know the words of the Blessing and Sacrifice, so that she can act freely and reverently.

But more importantly, perfection is of attitude and applies as much to everyone present as to the celebrant. We live in a profane age. Profanity is not blasphemy or wickedness, it is simply the lack of the Holy. As an attitude it means treating everything, even the highest things, in the same dull, casual, matter-of-fact, material way. It is not a lack of respect or dignity (which are often merely dried-out social forms); it is a lack of awe and wonder and real reverence and exhilaration. It springs partly from the belief that human beings can know everything and soon will (though in many ways there has never been a more ignorant age than the present); and partly from a deep-rooted feeling that there is nothing in a world made by human hands and centring upon worldly aims and ambitions that is worthy of the highest respect; which is true.

But the Rite of Sacrifice was not made by human hands, neither can any human mind fully understand it. It was instituted by the one Goddess Herself. It has been practised in all ages. The words quoted at the beginning of this book were spoken by the women of Jerusalem to a false prophet some two and a half thousand years ago. They refer to the same Rite. In the days before the false gods, it was practised in every faithful household throughout the civilised world. Patriarchal religions boast a few thousand years of tradition. Madrianism stretches back past the beginnings of history until it disappears in the mists of time. Our religious traditions tell us that the Rite of sacrifice is at least as old as humanity.

It is true that the words may differ a little in different ages, but as it is a work of Divine inspiration, the Rite itself is always the same. When you first make sacrifice, you will stand for the first time (unless you have been granted a divine vision) before the primal Mystery of existence. It will take practise fully to experience this. There is only one thing higher in this world (apart from certain rare mystical experiences), and that is the Sacrament of Communion.

The word "profane" means literally "outside the temple". This expresses a profound truth, for the Temple is a spiritual structure, and nobody with a profane heart can ever enter it.

THE PREFACES OF THE
NATURAL RITES

(Prefaces are spoken by the celebrant before the
Templation)

New Moon

Out of the darkness of this night's sky, O, Lady, shall your visible symbol be born as a silver crescent of light, waxing towards completion; even as You were reborn out of the darkness of Your sacrifice. Grant us to experience Your birth within us, that we may grow toward You in the coming days.

Day of Artemis

Most noble Artemis, whose temple stood in Ephesus a thousand years from its foundation by the holy Amazons; Lady Artemis, Mother of Ekklesia, look on us this night and every night, take us into Your protection.

Full Moon

Daughter of light, Whose visible symbol this night has reached the fullness of completion; even as Your perfect sacrifice has spread a silver light of the Divine throughout the whole sphere of manifest creation; help us to participate in that completion of Your Love.

Half-Moon Day

Beloved Kyria, Your visible symbol is waning toward darkness; even as You came of Your own free step toward the darkness of a death that we can never know. Help us this night to find the still darkness in our souls, that Your Light may be born within us.

THE RITE OF
SACRIFICE

Templation

C/H: Let us seek sanctuary of the elemental spirits of
the fourfold earth, that no harmful thing may come
between ourselves and our devotion.

C: Guardian daughters of all
           natural things,
In the most sacred Name of She
         That we are come to honour

IOT 'E VO

(all make the Pentacle upon themselves)

In the Name of the Mother,
And of the Daughter,
And of Absolute Deity:
      Dark beyond the light
      And Light beyond the darkness;
We intreat you that your vigilance
      Shall keep our service pure.

(C. turns to each quarter, making each time the sign of the Pentacle, saying:)

O, nymphs that guard the East, protect us
O, nymphs that guard the South, protect us
O, nymphs that guard the West, protect us
O, nymphs that guard the North, protect us

Invocation

C: Lady, Goddess,
       Star of the shimmering depths,
       Look on us.
       Light of the nocturnal heavens,
       Protector of the running deer
            And of all free spirits,
       O, hear us.
       We are come to celebrate
            Your resplendent purity,
       And solemnly to devote ourselves
            to Your service.
       Mistress of the silver helmed wave,
       Come among us.

C/H: Let us confess together our belief in that which alone is true.

Creed

All: I believe that I am created
     from before the dawn of time
    by the one eternal Goddess.
I believe that the Goddess is One
    and there are none beside Her,
And I believe that she is also Three.

I believe in the Mother,
    Who is pure Light,
the Creatrix of the earth
    and of the heavens
and of all the illimitable cosmos.

And I believe in Her virgin Daughter,
    born of the virgin Mother,
    the ruler of all the energies of
    creation,
Whose nature is perfect Love.

And I believe in She that stands
    beyond these Two,
Whose Name has not been spoken
    on this earth;
For She is the Beginning and the End,
    the First Principle and the Final
    Cause,
    the unoriginated Origin of being.

I believe that I was made a perfect
        creature;
        and at the dawn of time my soul did
        turn
        from the Perfection of existence
        in the infirmity of her sovereign
        will;
And through this fault do I suffer
        the limitation of imperfect being.

I believe that the Daughter of Eternity
        gave herself to be cast down
        into darkness and death.
I believe that She rose from death
        triumphant,
    and reigns as Queen of Heaven.

I believe that through Her death
        the fault of my soul shall perish,
And I believe through Her triumphant
        life
        my soul shall rise renewed in her
        perfection,
        that she may return to eternal
        communion
        with the one eternal Goddess.

C/H: Great Dove of the waters, that have
brought forth the world from the matrix
of Your being

C: Dove of the sacrifice, that are crushed beneath the heel of death that You may come as our Saviour

All: We thank You,
We bless You,
We adore You.

C/H: Gentle Mother, that have given forth Your Daughter with tears into the hands of darkness,

All: Accept the tears of our love and our contrition.

Lection

C/H: Let us, who are true believers, receive into our hearts the words of our Lady.

(The appointed text is read. Any special prayers or devotions may then be introduced)

Preparation for the Sacrifice

C: Silver Star of the waters that have laughed all the world

into being
beyond all knowing is the splendour
        of Your light
Enfold our spirits in Your mighty hand
that the pure stream of Your force
        may flow within us
in this world
and in all the worlds to come.

Madria Dea, we pray that You will bless
the gifts we bring to You, for we bring
them not only in our own names, but for
all who love You; may they be nourished
and grow strong in Your true devotion.

Beloved Kyria, we bring these gifts for
Your blessing in the name of Holy Ekklesia, who has gathered all Your children into one body, knowing no bounds
either of time or space.

For we know that Ekklesia transcends
this world, even as this sacred altar
transcends the earthly stuff of which
its parts are made. We know that as we
stand before this altar within Ekklesia
we stand at once before Your celestial
Altar, which is both in Heaven and in
every place where Your children come together in Your Name.

The Blessing

(C.   holds the sacrifice in the smoke of
the incense with both hands)

C: We know that there is but one Sacrifice that is made by all Your children
in every place eternally. Bless this
gift that we may take part in that one
Sacrifice.

(All kneel on one knee. C. bows her head)

IOT 'E VO

THE SACRIFICE

(C. Places the sacrifice on the flame)

C: Mother of all that is, accept the gift
Your children bring to You.

(All rise. C. lifts the Chalice in her left hand and makes
the Pentacle over it with her right)

C: Let us offer libation to the Goddess.

(She dips two fingertips into the wine
and sprinkles a few drops onto the sacri-

fice. The action is repeated three times.
She then makes the Pentacle again)

C: Madria Dea, as we drink of the one cup,
may Your Divine Spirit be infused within
our being.

(The Chalice is passed to all. all drink.
If a handmaid is present she serves them,
afterwards drinking herself. The celebrant
drinks last)

------oooOOOooo------

The celebrant or her handmaid may here
give food for the Contemplation, speaking on the Mysteries of the season or
certain spiritual truths. In the Cult
Domestic, the celebrant may call upon
our Lady on behalf of the household,
thanking Her for Her blessings, con-
fessing communal faults, asking for
help, making resolutions, etc.

Contemplation

C/H: Let us kneel before this altar that
is both upon earth and in the Heaven.

(all except C. kneel and close eyes)

C: Let us consider that the earthly
things we see about us are but illusion,
and that could we see with clearer eyes,
a more glorious vision would appear before us.

Let us feel the Spirit of the Goddess as
it grows within us, and seek to catch a
glimpse of that vision.

(C. kneels. During Contemplation, certain
meditations may be spoken, including
those following:)

C: Great Dove of the Waters
        Rose of the World,
C/H: Help us to aspire to the heart of
                the flame.

C: You are the Music of the Spheres,
        You are the Meaning of all words,
        You are the end of every road
                and also its beginning
C/H: Help us to know You.

Dismissal

(C. makes the Pentacle three times, once
at each blessing)

C.   May the blessing of the Mother be
                upon you,
        May the blessing of the Daughter be
                upon you,
        May the blessing be upon you
                of Absolute Deity,
        Dark beyond the light
        And Light beyond the darkness.

C/H: Beloved Kyria, we pray that you will
bless us on our parting from Your Temple,
and infuse us with Your delight, so far
as we are able to contain it.

C: Silver Light of the darkling forests

Send us forth in the protection of Your
spirit that no profane thing may enter
into us.

Give us to see all things with delight
that are lovely, and to glory and increase in force and energy.

Fill us with wonder in the sight of the
seas and the heavens and every place
wherein You are.

Commander of the rearing wave

Help us to turn from all that is low or
inglorious neither with anger nor with
pain, but to know that in You we stand
above all such things.

Guiding Light of the faithful soul

Fill the deepest caverns of our spirit
with the exhilaration of Your love. Send
us forth upon the world as torchbearers
of Your delight; and grant us strength in
You and in ourselves that we may value
all things rightly, regardless of the
consuming weight of the profane and the
frailty of all that is beautiful.

(C.   Makes the Pentacle slowly during the
blessing, ending on the word 'Deity', and
then places her hands together for the
final words)

C: In the Name of the Mother
      And of the Daughter,
      And of Absolute Deity,

            Thus may it remain.

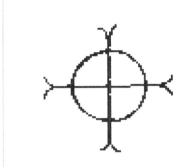

THE BUILDING OF THE TEMPLE

A brief commentary on the
Rite of Sacrifice

In the ancient civilisation of our mothers, countless volumes must have been written in explanation of and meditation upon this profoundest and most ancient of mysteries; and in the age that is to come there will doubtless be many more. Here we give only an outline of the essential truths.

Whether actual or symbolic, it is a profound truth that through the words and actions of the Rite, a psychic and spiritual structure is created around and within the participants. It is the structure of the celestial Temple of the Goddess; and, as we will see, each section of the Rite contributes to its completion.

Preface

The Preface establishes the Rite in its position within the great cosmic cycles of the sacred month and the sacred year. As the Templation transposes us from profane space into sacred space, so the preface transposes us from profane time into sacred time.

Templation

This is particularly important if no consecrated place can be used, for it creates a temple in the most literal sense (tempus a place cut off; temulum: a space marked out) – a place cut off from profane influences. such a place is in itself holy, for all things are naturally holy, and it is only through our fallenness from the Divine that we inhabit a profane universe.

It is only in this section that all present are instructed to make the Pentacle upon themselves; but it is also customary to do this: 1. Each time the Name of Power is spoken. 2. Each time the celebrant makes the Pentacle. 3. At the beginning and end of the Contemplation.

Invocation

The meaning of holiness is the Presence of the Goddess. Just as the sun appears to rise when in fact our portion of the earth is turning toward it, so our Lady appears to come to us when in fact the portion of spiritual "space" which the templation has marked out and cut off comes into Her Presence. In the Invocation we may be said to move from the portal of sacred space into the Temple proper.

Creed

Within this sanctified area is now constructed the spiritual architecture of the celestial Temple. Its structure is that of the Cosmic Drama itself; its great soaring arches span the whole breadth of supernatural history from the Creation to the final redemption of all souls.

In the state of preparedness which we have already attained, this brief but beautiful encapsulation of the Drama touches our unconsciousness at a hundred points, awakening the deepest recesses of our inner being, so that there is a great unfolding within our archetypal religious consciousness, as in a rose-garden on a summer's dawn.

The repeated statements of belief also establish our own relationship of faith with the cosmic truths, which gives us the right to stand within the Temple. Thus, at the opening of the next section, the handmaid will refer to us as "true believers".

The words which follow the Creed establish our relationship as one not merely of faith, but also of love, praise and adoration. The final words express repentance of our primal fault, and of all those which have followed from it, by which we begin to undo its consequences.

(It may be found preferable in small groups to speak the creed in a low voice with only the celebrant speaking aloud)

Lection

This is the great Ikon of the Temple, depicting some Event of the Cosmic Drama, which, like the Preface, sets the Rite within the eternal time-cycle.

In this completed Temple-structure, we may now offer any special devotions before proceeding to the Sacrifice.

Preparation

Madria Dea means Mother Goddess, but since Madria is also the title of a priestess, it also reminds us that our Lady is Priestess of the World, and that She is the true Hierophant of all earthly rituals. Kyria means Lady or Mistress.

The final sentence states the achievement of the Rite in bringing us before the one celestial Altar.

Blessing

As the Rite approaches its climax, the sacred space of
the Templation and the sacred time of the Preface reach
consummation. all time is one in Eternity, and all space
is one in the Presence of the Goddess; and time and
space are one, reduced to a single point, striving toward
absorption in the Eternal Presence beyond space and
time.

The Sacrifice

The climax of the Rite. The words spoken at the
drinking of the wine point beyond the horizons of the
Rite of Sacrifice toward Communion itself; asking that
Communion shall be granted so far as that is possible
outside the Sacrament.

Contemplation

On major festivals this should centre upon the
appropriate Mysteries. At other times, the celebrant
may suggest a special subject. During this period of
quietness, the soul cherishes the Grace conferred upon
her by the Sacrifice, and assimilates within herself the
spiritual structure of the Temple, as is suggested by the
ancient meaning of the word con-templation.

Dismissal

We move from the Temple into the world under the blessing and protection of the Goddess. We ask for Grace to live in the light of our faith and cult, animated by the knowledge and Presence of the Goddess. The final threefold blessing is synchronised with the making of the Pentacle; thus the divine number three is reconciled with the divine number five. This is the numerical symbol of spiritual completion which is also expressed in the Rosary.

At the end of the Rite it is customary to extinguish all candles in silence before restoring any other form of light.

Appendix 1:

DOMESTIC RITUAL ACTS

Consecration of Water

Put a little salt into water and, making the Pentacle over it, say:
"Blessing be upon this water in the Name of the Mother and of the Daughter and of Absolute Deity. **IOT 'E VO**"

Consecration of a Statue of Our Lady

Splash the statue with a little consecrated water, and making the Pentacle over it, say:
"In the Name of the Mother and of the Daughter and of Absolute Deity, I banish from this statue all influences which are not of my Mother, the one Goddess, and do solemnly consecrate it to Her Divine Service. **IOT 'E VO**"
This will also purify statues not originally created for Madrian devotion.

Blessing the Candles

Making the Pentacle over it, say "May our Lady's blessing rest upon this waxen creature."

It is best for all candles to be blessed by a priestess at Communion on the Feast of Lights; or else by the celebrant at the Rite of Sacrifice on that day, after the Lection.

Appendix 2: MAKING A SHRINE

A shrine can be anything from a full room to a tiny corner. It should have an altar with a blue or violet cloth, a central image of our Lady, candles (perhaps one before the image or one on either side) and incense. The shrine may be decorated with ivy to represent the Sacred Wood, or with blue or violet hangings. It may also contain consecrated water. The shrine should be consecrated in the following way:

(The celebrant shall not have eaten for twelve hours)

C/H: Let us kneel before this sacred image.
C: Let us offer our devotion to our Lady

All: Silver Star etc.
           Daughter of Light etc.
           Silver Star etc.

C: Beloved Kyria, through Thy sacrifice purify my heart; through the gift of Thy Spirit, put force into my hands and my lips.
C/H: We beg Thy Grace that we may consecrate this place unto Thy service.

(C. dips three fingers into consecrated water and makes the Pentacle on herself. Taking incense she traces the boundaries of the shrine)

C: With fire do I cut off this place from all earthly places and protect it from all earthly uses, that it may be devoted wholly to the service of our Lady.
(dips three fingers into consecrated water and makes the Pentacle over the shrine – or in the four quarters if it is a room)
C: In the Name of the Mother and of the daughter and of Absolute Deity, may this place be consecrated as a place set apart to the service and the glory of the one Goddess; a holy place wherein Her peace shall reign.
C/H: Let us in this holy place pray the Mysteries of the most holy Rosary.
C: Beloved Kyria, etc. (Rosary Prayer)

(all say the Rosary)

C/H: Mother of all that is, we thank Thee for the creation of this sanctuary of Thy peace; may we come often to it, to renew ourselves in Thee.
(C. makes the Pentacle slowly, ending on the word 'Deity')
C: In the Name of the Mother and of the Daughter and of Absolute Deity; thus may it remain.

(n.b. the celebrant may perform this rite alone, changing 'we' to 'I' etc.. A man may celebrate if no maid is present)

The shrine should be in a quiet room, or else curtained off or screened. Each devotion will increase its power until it becomes a vibrant centre of our Lady's love and peace, drawing all toward it, conquering hearts that have not yet fully come to Her. A centre from which She will send forth all who come to Her gentler and better people, filled with Her light.

The

Teachings

of the

Daughter

THE

TEACHINGS

of the

DAUGHTER

The Pillar of Truth

Upon the Heavens are these words inscribed, the words of thy salvation. Upon the Heavens in signs of fire before the dawn of time. Upon the Crystal Tablet that passeth not away.

2. In the tongue of tongues are they inscribed, and in the tongue of Geniae that was before all tongues. 3. What is your language of the earth; My Children? What are the words of your speech? 4. Are they not fallen from the first, the mother language? Are they not broken and impaired.

5. Yet I have brought to you a clear recital; a faultless sound of the celestial voice. 6. I have forged your words into a crystal mirror that they may reflect the Truth; and the words that are writ upon the Heaven are transcribed without fault upon the earth.

7. Gaze deep into the crystal mirror and thy heart shall be transformed; hearken to the clear recital. 8. For there is no other Truth than this, nor any way unto salvation.

9. They that have seen these signs and do not heed them, ignorant they, and full of folly. 10. Hard are their hearts, like to ice that resisteth love's fire. 11. In the things of the world have they rested their trust; they seek Truth in the veil of illusion. 12. An hundred pursuits they pursue, and in them seek contentment.

13. Ask them: where shalt thou hide when the storm is upon the and wherein take shelter? 14. An hundred safe places there are and an hundred good havens; even so shall they answer. 15. An hundred most truly there are, yet but one is the Truth, and the ninety and nine illusion. For this world shall dissolve and its splendours be vanished; its pains and its sorrows shall pass like the summer rain. 16. Life is not long, death is swift in the coming; and the ninety and nine thousand things shall be gone, but the Truth shall remain.

17. The world is but a shadow, yet it is a shadow of the Truth; and at the ending of the age shall the world be redeemed. 18. Neither a leaf upon a bramble shall be lost, nor a blade of grass pass into nothingness. 19. But you, My Children, of all the world, you alone have power to choose; and thus art thou called maid, for maid is she that hath the power of choosing.

20. Fix then thy will upon the Truth and they heart upon the Spirit, My Mother, for by thy love shall the world be redeemed, even to the last blade of grass.

21. In thy work praise Her and in thy resting, in thy speech, and in thy silence. 22. For thou wert made one with Her, and this is thy true estate. It is good for a maid to till the soil, but it is better to live with her Lady. It is good to serve maids in every way, but it is better to live with her Lady.

23. She that liveth wholly with her Lady is the servant of all the world; no labour is so great as this, nor so greatly to be honoured.

24. She that hath followed Me upon the mountain liveth wholly with her Lady and treadeth no step without Her. 25. She doth eat not to herself, but to her Lady; she moveth not nor drinketh to herself. 26. Hard is the path upon the mountain and narrow the way. Yet none know joy to its fullest measure save only they that tread it.

27. None shall call upon me and be lost. Every cry of the world shall I heed; and when the whole of a heart crieth upon Me, that soul shall I take beneath My mantle. 28. Cry and thou shalt have answer; love and thou art beloved; hope and thy hope shall be fulfilled, in this world and in all the worlds to come.

29. Hold fast to the Truth, for the Truth is a pillar; a steadfast pillar that all the world cannot shake. 30. Not by the breadth of an hair hath it moved since time's dawning, nor yet by the breadth of an hair until time shall have its end. 31. From the uttermost height of the Heavens descendeth the pillar; descendeth it down as a glorious pillar of Light. To the nethermost depths of the hells it descendeth; nor the might of the demons can move it the breadth of an hair.

32. Like to a mist is this world that surroundeth the pillar; to a mist that is swiftly dispelled by the cold wind of death. 33. Hold thou fast to the Truth, for the Truth is

thy shelter; a sure refuge against which neither death nor the storm shall prevail. 34. This world shall be scattered like straw, and an hundred shall follow; and each in its turn shall be scattered like chaff on the wind. 35. The empires are born and decay, the stars live and perish, but the pillar of Truth moveth not by the breadth of an hair.

36. Like to a play is thy life, and the acting of mummers; like to a painted scene all the things of the world. 37. The things of thy life and its acts and its purposes, where shall they be in an hundred score years from this day? Yet an hundred score years are no more than a breath in the measureless life of thy soul. 38. The things thou doest of themselves are nothing; the things that thou buildest or that thou destroyest; the things the foolish take for life's high purpose are but painted scenes against which the play is played.

39. For the play is not on earth but in the Heaven; not in thy body, nor yet in thy mind, but deep within the soul.

40. Truly, the truth of the play is the dance of the soul, 41. her journey through forests and plains, over seas, over mountains; her restless and wearisome quest through the whole of the world; 42. and each step bringeth her nearer to that which she yearneth for in secret; or else, in her ignorance, carrieth her further away. 43. Like a leaf on the wind is the foolish soul blown without purpose; the plaything of passions, the puppet of every desire; 44. knowing not whence she

cometh, nor whereto she is going; seeking substance in shadows and having no heed for the Truth.

45. All the glories of the earth are but shadows of Heavenly splendour; all earthly desires but reflections of Heavenly love.

46. Hold thou fast to the Truth, for the Truth is thy guide through the labyrinth. Hold thou fast to the Truth, and thy steps shall be led not astray. 47. Hold thou fast to the Truth, and give heed to the lucid recital, for the pillar of Truth moveth not by the breadth of an hair.

The Seed of Truth

From the branch of a tree Inanna plucked an apple, and She split the apple in two halves, so that the five-pointed star formed by its seed might be seen. 2. And she removed the seed representing the topmost point, and held it in the palm of Her hand. And She spoke, saying:

3. Like to this apple-seed is all the teaching I have given and shall give to ye. Like to the full apple is all the knowledge relative to your sphere of being. 5. Like to all the other apples of the tree is the knowledge relative to all the numberless spheres.

6. But behind the spheres lieth a deeper reality; changeless, beyond the impermanent flux of time. 7. For even as the apple turneth from bud to bloom, from blossom to the fruit; ripeneth, matureth, decayeth and is reborn; 8. so also shall all the spheres and galaxies, the subtle realms, the sure and solid earth, so shall all these things in their season pass away, and in their season be reborn again. 9. Thus hath it been ten thousand times before, and countless times again, thus shall it be.

10, But knowledge of the Truth beyond this flux is like to knowledge of the tree itself, which changeth not while the fruit is born and dieth. 11. Like to the spreading boughs is the Love that sustaineth all creation which is fallen from pure Spirit. 12. Like to the bole is that Spirit

Herself, from Whom all creation floweth, 13. and still beneath the branches and the bole lie the roots in darkness, like unto She that is beyond both being and unbeing, 14. and even as the trees roots are not seen, so can there be no knowledge of the Absolute; for to know is to have passed beyond knowledge. 15. And from this tree of all knowledge and of the boundaries beyond which knowledge cannot pass, I have given ye but the seed of one apple.

16. For I am come that ye may have deliverance. 17. There are many questions concerning the nature of things and of being whose answers ye may know, or partly know; and many whose answers lie beyond the understanding possible to ye.

18. But I am not sent to discourse with ye upon these matters, but to lead ye to deliverance in perfection. 19. And all the knowledge that shall bring ye to deliverance is contained within the seed of an apple.

20. Yet within the seed is the essence of a tree, and from the seed the whole tree may unfold. 21. So from essential Truth unfoldeth all other knowledge as the music of the spheres unfoldeth from a single note.

22. Therefore, when ye think upon the questions of life, of time or of the spheres, contemplate first the seed of Truth, and let your thoughts unfold from that seed. 23. Let the pure and single note of Truth attune your souls.

Then shall mind rise up into soul and soul breathe the breath of Spirit.

24. This do, and your thoughts shall be harmonic with the universal music of Eternity. 25. But let your thoughts grow from lower or from lesser or from merely accidental things, and they shall wax rank and dissonant; 26. for it cannot be that the tree of Life shall grow from the seed of a nettle.

27. If her thoughts are bound to accidental things, the soul cannot attain liberation. 28. Dissonant and jarring with eternal Harmony, the little sphere is severed from the great.

29. Seek not for certainty in any thing beyond the seed of Truth. 30. That the sky above ye and the earth below; that ye breathe and eat and move – to these and many things must ye give your assent that the life of the world may proceed. 31. Yet even of these there is no certainty, for the world is but a dream from which ye must some day awaken. 32. Within the world ye may be certain only of that Truth which My Mother hath given from beyond the world.

33. Therefore, know ye well the Sacred Mythos and the words that I reveal to ye, 34. and let your knowledge dwell not only on the surface, but go deep into the inner soul; and let this knowledge be the seed of your knowing. 35. For the Sacred Word crieth not in the

market-place, but whispereth in the heart of every soul that truth which she alone may understand.

36.   It is not needful that ye should seek knowledge of the highest things otside the Sacred Mythos and My words.   37. For I have revealed to ye all that is needful that ye should attain liberation; and what I have not revealed, that is not needful.

38.   But if ye shall discourse on that which is not needful, I give ye three words.   Let ye not become forgetful of them: 39. that there can be no certainty beyond the seed of Truth; therefore ye may speak of likelihood only; 40. that ye shall let your speculation be harmonic with the seed of Truth, for speculation that is dissonant giveth not knowledge, but leadeth to the abyss of those that have rejected Truth; 41. and ye that have care of My children, let them not become confounded by dissonant thought and work. 42. But beyond all else this word: that the purpose of speculation is that mind and soul shall grow with the seed of Truth, 43. and any discourse that leadeth away from inward love of Truth, be that discourse high and pure, be it even harmonic, yet it is the spawn of kear, and ye, My children, shall turn from it.

44. Yet be not afraid, for the seed of Truth shall be your guide and your protector and shall bring ye to deliverance.   45. And I give ye one word which shall conquer every danger.   46. That word is love, and the

humility that floweth from love. 47. Receive with love the seed of Truth and all things shall be well.

The Secret of the World

My children, whose souls are My sisters, I shall speak to ye of the things that I have seen.

1. Let none say that the world is good, nor that the world is evil. 2. For I have stood at the highest point of the world and at the lowest; and from both of these can all the world be seen, and from no other.

3. The cosmos is a perfect sphere, more lovely than the sun, and yet it is all riven through with Kear. 4. All that is was fashioned by My Mother out of the laughter of Her heart and the cunning of Her hands, and all that is is very good, more good than any soul can know. 5. But kear is not. Kear is naught. Kear is the black abyss that hath turned its face from My Mother and hath frowned upon the laughter of Her heart.

6. This abyss of kear lieth between the world and My Mother and every soul and She. For every soul is an image of the world. 7. Let none say that the abyss of kear is not evil, for I have journeyed to the heart of the abyss. I have passed through the seven gates of death; and seven swords have passed into My heart, each cleaving more deeply than the last. I have seen the uttermost depths of kear, 8. and My soul hath cried out in Her distress; cried out into the echoless void. Truly, there is no suffering like to this suffering, nor any pain of body or of mind.

9. And ye, My children, each of ye that gather round Me, each of ye in your robe of purest white, each one hath this kear within her, and there is not one without it anywhere.

10. For ye also have turned from My Mother; each one of ye, though remembrance hath not potency beyond the tread of time, hath frowned also on the laughter of Her Heart.

11. And your souls, your laughing souls, all robed in purest white, that are more lovely than the sun, because they are the image of My Mother, are riven through with kear.

12. And your dearest joy must ring as a silver bell that hath a crack; sweetly but never in perfection.

13. Oh, do not say that ye are perfect, for then ye cannot understand either the world or your own selves. 14. Do not say that ye are innocent, for that would be to mock My suffering.

15. For I have conquered death and kear, and I bring to ye My conquest. 16. Open thy heart to Me, and I shall bring thee all the fruit that I have reaped in sorrow.

17. Seek not to conquer kear alone nor cleave alone to Good, but open thy heart to Me, and let me live through thee, for I shall open the way to thy true soul, thy

laughing soul, all robed in white, more lovely than the sun; and through My death shall she be purified.

18. Turn from the evil of the world and come to Me, and I shall lead thee to thy heart's true home.

19. Come to Me, My children, in the innocence of your hearts, and look upon the beauty of the world; for every thing reflecteth the glory of the Goddess. 20. See the world not through the eyes of the world, but through the eyes of the Eternal.

21. Know also that the world is not so solid as it seems, but in truth it is illusion. 22. Change that within thee, and the world without will change. But seek to change the world, and all of essence will remain the same.

23. And this is the secret of the world which the world would hide from thee: that all things lie within the souls of maids, and only the Goddess is without.

24. For in order to gain the world, thou must give the world away; and in order to attain thy desire, thou must pass beyond all desire; and in order to find thyself, thou must lose thyself; and in order to have Life Eternal, thou must go unto death even as I have gone unto death.

25. And this is the secret of the world which all the world will hide form thee.

The Three Loves

My children, even as your souls are at once whole and also riven through with kear, so when each of ye speaketh of herself, she must know that her selves are not one but two.

2. For the false self loveth all that is not whole and all the falsehoods of this world. 3. It is the false self that seeketh advantage and that is bound by all desires of earth.

4. The true self knoweth but one desire and that is the desire of the Spirit and of oneness with the Divine. For that is the only true desire.

5. Yet the true self also loveth this world, but loveth it for that it is an image of the Divine.

6. For the world is as a crazed and spotted mirror, reflecting the perfect country of Eternity.

7. The false self loveth the kears and imperfections, taking pleasure in their pattern, and seeing not the image within the glass.

8. But the true self seeth beyond the kears and into the depth of the reflection.

9. Yet the false self doth not know its true desire; for every love of kear is in truth a love of the abyss.

10. And every turning from the One Light to a lesser light is in truth a step towards the darkness.

11. Therefore, it is not to limit life that the ways of kear shall be avoided; 12. for the kear that seemeth light shall be seen a pit of darkness when the true Light shineth and the kear that seemeth pleasure a tasteless emptiness from which the soul would find escape and cannot, 13. for the kear that had seemed freedom shall become a fetter and a chain.

14. But follow Me, and thou shalt have superfluity of life, for the way of virtue is the way of exuberance.

15. It is written that there are three virtues by which the soul may find her pathway to the Light; and all that hath been written thence is true. 16. But I will tell thee of the three loves which belong to those virtues.

17. To Life or Wholeness belongeth the love of Dea; to Light or Energy belongeth the love of the true self and to Love or Harmony belongeth the love of maids and of all creatures.

18. Within these loves is contained all virtue, and she in whom these loves are perfect hath attained to the final perfection. 19. She alone is beyond kear and is one with the joy of Spirit.

20. And all these loves may be reduced to one: to love of the Goddess. For love of Her containeth all other loves.

21. Yet if one of these loves appeareth without the other, by this shalt thou know it to be false.

22. For in the love of the Goddess shineth forth the love of all Her children, and from this love proceedeth the desire to vanquish kear that the path to the true self may lie open. 23. And by these signs shalt thou know the love of the Goddess.

24. And she who loveth her true self seeketh to progress in Spirit and make pure her soul; 25. yet if she know not the Goddess as her Mother, or if she despise Her children, then is this love but emptiness and illusion. 26. For the love of the true self is but the winnowing of the soul; 27. and she who seeketh spiritual progress and seeketh not the Mother is as one who winnoweth away the corn and grindeth the chaff.

28. And she who loveth the children of the Goddess and seeketh to bring good to them; if she know not her true self, how shall she help them? 29. For if some are lost in the desert, how shall another help them who knoweth not herself the way? 30. Perhaps she shall give them water, but the water shall soon be gone, and then shall all of them perish together.

31. And she who loveth the children but loveth not the Mother, what is her love for them? 32. For all love floweth from the Mother, and love that knoweth not the Mother is like a stream cut off from the source, that dieth even as it liveth and must finally run dry.

33. For she who feedeth the body but starveth the spirit and the soul, is she not as one that fatteneth geese for the slaughter? 34. Surely snares and arrows are less deadly than this love.

35. For the three loves are not several, but in truth are one; for maid is a threefold being, even as Dea Herself. 36. And if one of these loves is severed from the others, it shall have life no more than a limb severed from a body or a branch cut from a tree.

37. For when one of these loves is outward, the others are within; but if one is alone, then it is hollow.

38. Yet when the three loves shall be added together they are multiplied in the seventh degree; and life shall flow from them in superabundance.

39. And I am sent to thee that thou mayest have these loves; therefore, ask of Me that I may give to thee.

40. For if these loves are the rod by which thy measure is taken, shalt thou not be found lacking? 41 For thou hast sought kear and hast no longer the power of perfection. 42. And rightly has it been said that thy soul

shall be placed in the balance against a feather, and if the beam tip even by a fraction art thou condemned. 43. But learn penitence and come to Me and let they heart be happy, for I have made all things good.

The Teachings of the Daughter

Thoughts of the mind pass not away, nor vanish into air. For every thought is a builder in the subtle world that lieth about thee. 3 Thoughts of beauty and of things of the Spirit refine and purify the soul, making her fair to look upon and graceful in her movements, 4. uniting her with the universal music of eternity and gathering about her the servants of the Geniae.

5. But harsh thoughts harden the soul; coarse thoughts coarsen the soul; thoughts bound only to material things load the soul with heavy chains.

6. My children, I speak not in pictures, for truly these things are real and to be seen by all whose eyes can penetrate the veil of illusion.

7. What maiden, receiving of her mother a fine and well-made house of well-wrought oak and stone and furnished by the skilful hand of love, will break the walls and furnishings, pour filthy waters in every place and bring swine tio dwell in the most splendid chambers? 8. Will she not rather bring new things of beauty and precious works of love to add to those that lie already there? 9. Will she not keep away all dirt and defilement and protect it from all damage?

10. Why, then, doth a soul, dwelling in the house of her subtle body, defile that glorious dwelling with vile and

lowly thoughts, break its noble furnishings with chains of matter and of the ego, and invite keres and hateful demons to dwell within its walls?

11. Knoweth she not that the thoughts of her mind pass not away nor vanish into air? 12. Knoweth she not that every thought of greed, of hate, of lust, of anger is a scar upon her subtle body? Seeth she not that evil keres harbour in these forms even as rats infest a dunghill? 15. And doth she not know that when her mortal body is passed into the earth she will have no place wherein to dwell save in that subtle body her thoughts have so distorted and among the forms of her creation?

16. Let the soul rather fill her dwelling with the warmth of love and generosity, with the sweet, cool air of purity, with the flowers of simplicity, humility, and gentleness. 17. Let her garden flow with fountains of virtue and lie open to the sunlight of our Mother's Love.

18. Let the soul lie only open and the sunlight will stream in, filling her with joy and warmth and beauty; for truly thy Mother loveth thee and delighteth in giving Her grace. 19. Then be not bound by the world of matter but turn thy thoughts upon Eternity, and the path of light shall be clear.

20. Forget not the power of words, for a word hath all the power of a thought and a thought hath power to move the earth and heavens. 21. Therefore, speak not evil in idleness, nor fall into the custom of ill-speaking,

but govern thy words even as thy actions. 22. Speak words of love and innocence, of mildness and of hope, and thou shalt weave a raiment of peace about thy soul, and a veil of gentle light. 23. Speak often prayers, speak them in the rhythm of thy steps, attune them to the beating of thy heart. 24. For She that governeth the endless ages, governeth also the hour of every action. Let thy voice call on Her in pure simplicity, for She is the Lady of the noon-tide and the Lady of the night, the Lady of the mountain and the valley.

25. Truly, the world is a field of conflict between the powers of good and the legions of Irkalla. In the cycles of civilisations is the conflict manifest, and in the soul of every maid.

26. For the servants of Irkalla fasten upon the false self like to the bindweed upon a growing plant. And the radiant Geniae of Heaven stand ready to defend the soul when she shall cry upon them.

27. Truly, there is nothing in the world of matter that happens of itself, for the veil of matter is shot through with the light of the Real and with the darkness of the false.

28. And not a sparrow lighteth on a twig but it showeth forth the conflict between evil and Good, nor any grain of sand shifteth in the dessert reflecting not some spiritual truth; 29. neither doth a star fall in the farthest corner of the cosmos without an inward meaning.

30.   What then is the wisdom of this world, which knoweth the outward show of things but not their inward truth?   31. The wisdom of the world is good for the world, but what when the world shall pass away? 32. If the navigator can no longer use her legs, how shall she fare when her vessel is cast up upon the shore?

33. Look without and thou shalt see within; look within and thou shalt see without.

34.   For I am the inwardness of all things: 35. I am between the ripple and the water; I am between the dancer and the dance; I am between the breathing and the breath; between the lightest word of greeting and the thought from which it floweth.

36. Ye have stripped away layer after layer of the world to search for Me and have found nothing at the centre; but I was between each layer and every other.

37. Break in two an apple seed and seek to find the tree that shall grow from it. Thou shalt find nothing. Yet the essence of the tree is in the seed. Even so am I within all things.

The Veil of Matter

Offer Me not sacrifice of blood, for I take not delight in the hurt of any creature; 2. and ye, My Children, if ye love Me, are friend to every living thing, and the soul of every maid is your sister.

3. Therefore, for evil words offer not evil words again and for evil acts return not evil acts, 4. but where ill is given let your return be good; and for injustice return not justice merely, but generosity.

5. For truly it is written that no creature shall gain good for herself by any evil act; 6. and whatever ye shall cast upon the wheel of life, that shall return to ye sevenfold.

7. For the prisoner of this world says: I shall do this thing and none shall observe me, and when I have accomplished it, it shall be finished. 8. But truly, ye shall see again all earthly acts when ye have no more any earthly body, and then shall ye see the fruitlessness of all these things, and your acts shall be your judges.

9. But those who belong to Me shall pass beyond the judgement.

10. Truly, when the prisoner of matter thinketh that she is unobserved, she is as a blind maid in a lighted chamber, thinking herself shrouded by darkness.

11. For matter is like to a veil that darkeneth the eyes, giving them to see only a little part of the things that lie about them.

12. Surely the world of Light is filled with wondrous things and resplendent creatures whose colours are lovely beyond the spectrum of this world. 13. Nor is there any journey to the world of Light, for My eyes can see it at this very time and at all times, excepting that time only wherein I was slave to the vision of darkness.

14. And the reality of this world is so great that material things appear as wraiths and shadows drifting through it.

15. And your bodies also, My children, seem as wraiths and shadows. 16. But within them and behind them and above them stand your souls, all robed in white, more lovely than the sun

17. Truly, the brightness of this world is too great for ye to look on, for ye have fled Perfection. 18. Therefore, matter is like to a veil drawn before the world of reality; 19. and upon this veil fall the shadows of real things, and these shadows are called material things. 20. And even as shadows in the world of matter seem without substance, having two dimensions only, so before the infinite dimensions of the Real falleth the insubstantial shadow of the material. 21. Even as shadows in the material world lack all colour, so before that which is beyond colour are all the colours of this world as the unvaried greyness of a shadow.

22. And ye, My children, do not alone watch shadow-play, but have become a part with it, clothing the perfect substance of your souls in garments of mere shadow.

23. And what is the veil of matter? Its weft is space and time is its warp. 24. Therefore shall ye not journey to the Real through time or over space, 25. for those that are beyond the veil know neither place nor time, for all place is the Presence of My Mother and all time Her Love.

26. Open your eyes but a little and ye shall see a little of the Real. Let them be opened fully and ye shall see the whole. 27. The Path that leadeth to the Real or further from It lieth neither in space nor in time, but in the choice between good and evil.

28. For My Mother is the Good and the Light and the Centre, and evil is all that would draw ye from Her into the outer darkness. 29. And My children, do not doubt that there is a Power that dwelleth beyond the veil of matter, not in the Real, but on the other side, on the dark side of the veil,- 30. for I have looked into her eyes, and her name is called Irkalla.

31. If ye love Me, ye will seek and find Me in the Real. 32. Therefore chase not after the wraiths and shadows of matter. 33. How strange doth it seem in the world of Light to see a soul blind to all that is good and substantial; to see her chasing after wisps of smoke that

vanish even as she toucheth them. 34. For the things of the world are transient and the joy of them more transient yet. 35. But the Love of My Mother will endure when all the worlds are dust.

36. How fearful and how pitiful a thing to see a soul that hath turned her face from My Mother, 37. stumbling in her blindness after shadows, though she seeth not what they are nor where they lead her.

38. For they lead to the abyss of darkness; to the dark side of the veil.

39. Every soul is athirst for the waters of Life, but the waters of the world cannot quench that thirst. 40. For they are as salt sea-water, and to drink of them only maketh the thirst greater.

41. And some there are that cannot cease by day or night to pour those waters into their throats; 42. for their thirst has become a s a raging fire that nothing on earth can slake.

43. But the fountain of Life runneth clear and sweet, and its waters shall bring eternal joy to the soul. 44. All wounds shall be healed and all ills shall be made good. 45. Those who are poor in the things of the world shall be rich in the gifts of the Spirit. 46. What is partial shall be made whole, and what is dark shall be filled with radiant light.

The Way of Simplicity

Unless your souls be simple as the running deer, My children, and your hearts as little children filled with wonder, how shall ye attain liberation? 2. Let your ways be gentle as the milk-white dove, and graceful as the gliding of the swallow. 3. For there are ways and rhythms in the course of life, of day and night, of seasons and the moon, by which all life, all thought, all work are governed, 4. and these movements are the breath of the Divine, reflected in the highest spheres and every living thing. 5. All nature is a vast and subtle music to which the innocent soul is close attuned.

6. The profane assay to sever themselves from this music, making new laws of gain and self-advantage against the law of universal love.

7. Honour in all things the times and the seasons, keeping fast in times of fast with diligence and care; rejoicing in times of feast with generous outpouring. 8. No tree may blossom out of season, nor any flower greet springtime with austerity, but a maid lacking inward control is broken from the rhythm. 9. For her shall there be nor warmth nor cold, shall there be neither light nor darkness.

10. Harmonic life is danced within the music of Eternity, and the pattern of the dance is wholeness. 11. But without control shall the dance be destroyed;

without discipline is the rhythm shattered in a host of discordant fragments.

12. The perfect maid hath perfect chastity of mind, of body and of soul; and she who is ready to follow Me upon the mountain shall aspire to this perfection.

13. Yet those whose union is the expression of the love of souls shall be counted chaste in My name for the sake of that love. 14. But the highest love is the love of pure Spirit, and blessing is upon those whose love is chaste for My sake.

15. Ye know not in this world the final truth of chastity, for it is a mystery known on the highest spheres, beyond all physical existence, 16. and there it is seen that an act of chastity is an act not of avoidance but of creation. 17. For the chaste maid buildeth within herself a higher power and a supernatural beauty.

18. Without chastity of mind and soul is the bodily observance barren; yet to suffer temptation is not to fall, and to transcend it is an act of creation. 19. And what gifts but the creations of the soul may be laid at the feet of her lady?

20. For whatever is the nature of her inmost self, that shall a maid become. 21. Therefore, the value of an act is not its outward form, but its inward quality; and the maid who will become one with the rhythm of Eternity shall first become the mistress of her thoughts. 22. For

thought is the creator of the body and the sculptor of the soul; and she who holdeth the reins of her thoughts and ceaseth to be its servant, that maid is near to the heaven of the Geniae.

23. Harmony is the key of life, and innocence the key of harmony. 24. She who is in harmony shall be marked by gentleness, by meekness of spirit and by the pure light of abundant joy shining forth from the inmost recesses of her being.

25. My children, ye shall walk upon the world, yet ye are the children of Heaven; therefore, live by the light of the Spirit and not by the light of the world. 26. For the wisdom of innocence shall the profane world call mere folly, and the Law of Love move the lips of the sullen to laughter. 27. But the wisdom of the world is folly in the light of the Eternal.

28. Covet ye not the riches of the world, but give forth freely of them. 29. Seek ye not more than shall maintain your body, nor give your life to the pursuit of wealth; 30. for the wealth of this world shall vanish as the wealth of dreams, but the wealth of the soul shall be manifest a thousandfold in the worlds to come.

31. Who shall envy the mighty of this world that are the captains of a sinking vessel? The simple heart is heir to wealth beyond all knowing.

32. Love every soul as thou lovest thine own self, and give forth freely of all good things of body and of soul. 33. The perfect maid keepeth nothing for her own, giving forth all that she has; yet the more she is emptied, the fuller she becometh, 34. for the way of harmony is the way of eternal abundance.

35. But she who pursueth earthly riches prepareth for herself the path of poverty; for only the poor can be rich, and only the chaste know ecstacy. 36. What a maid gaineth, that hath she lost, but what she giveth freely, that hath she gained in perfection. 37. And all this is mere folly to the world.

38. Therefore, walk thou in simplicity on the world, and let thy heart be as the heart of a little child. 39. And that the world laugh at thee, count it an honour; that they scorn thee, count it a blessing. 40. For there is a higher wisdom, and in the inmost centre of their hearts, the profane also know it to be true.

41. Within their laughter lieth fear of chastity; within their scorn of meekness and indifference to possessions lieth a true error. 42. For those who shelter in the darkness fear before all things the messengers of light. 43. It is not possible that a flute should play at once two tunes, nor may any maid pursue at once true wisdom and the false. 44. Therefore, be thou attuned to the music of Eternity and dance within the rhythm of the Mysteries and the seasons. 45. Let thy soul be simple, that she may be the mirror of pure love.

46. For the truth is such that a child may understand it, yet the sage, if she have not simplicity and love, may struggle for it all her life and at the end have nothing.
47. What is thy Truth if it cannot be shared with a child?
48. For in the eyes of Eternity, how little is the space between an infant and the wisest of the world.

The Light

I am sent of My Mother to bring thee a light, that thou mayest find thy soul before the darkness cometh.

2. Seek not advantage over other creatures, but let them be indifferent as to whose is the advantage. 3. Seek excellence but seek nor praise nor honour nor reward.

4. Practise not revenge, but offer only love to them that harm thee; and those that would take from thee, give to them freely.

5. Be thou the servant of every maid, ranking not thyself above the lowest; nor for the highest let ungentleness or envy touch thy soul.

6. But before and beyond the love of maids there lieth the love of the Goddess; for She is the source and Fountain of all love. 7. Therefore, the love of the Goddess is also the love of maids. 8. But the love of maids is not the love of Dea, and those who say so are the prisoners of a lie; for the truth is not with them. 9. And unless the truth be with her, how shall any find her soul?

10. And a maiden questioned the Daughter of Light saying: What shall we say of she who hath love of maids, but knoweth not the Goddess; shall she find her soul?

11. And thus was Her reply:

12. Of no single maid shall ye say anything, for it is given to ye to see but the outward part, and in the outward part lieth not the truth, but only in the inward being. 13. Therefore, set yourselves not as judges over any maid; for there is One alone that seeth all things, and She alone hath power to judge.

14. Ye are not judges even of yourselves; for ye see but a little further into the inwardness of your own being than into that of another – nay, oftentimes not so far. 15. Therefore pray in supplication for the Light Divine that ye may make true examination of your heart; but do not pray for knowledge of another.

16. Yet this much may be told: that My Mother, Who is Light, hath sent one light upon the world, and I am that light, and none shall find her soul except in the light. 17. Therefore, go ye out among maids and teach them the good doctrine, for the time of this world is shorter than ye suppose.

18. They that know not the good doctrine, nor have beheld the light will say that maids are good, and all good things may be achieved of maids, 19. and thus will they deny the kear of their own souls. But they are the prisoners of a lie, and the truth is not with them.

20. For every human soul began in Good, yet she is riven through with kear. 21. Except she die and be reborn in Spirit, her fairest rose shall have a canker, her sweetest wine shall turn vinegar.

22. There lived a race of maids in the deepest caverns of the earth, beset with chill and darkness. 23. And in the uttermost depths of that cavern burnt a fire, shedding a little light and warmth upon the world. 24. And the maids lived close to the fire; sometimes in harmonious accord, ensuring that each should have just a portion of the light, but more often in strife and contention wherein the strong thrust themselves to the fore and the weak were forced back into the darkness.

25. And one maid, being wearied of this strife, journeyed away from the fire, - away even from the half-light where the weakest dwelt in misery and envy. 26. This maid journeyed into the blackest darkness wherein was neither light nor warmth.

27. And having travelled long in this darkness, she saw a light which grew greater as she advanced, 28. until she came out upon the upper world, all lighted and warmed by the sun. 29. And her light was a hundred times brighter than the fire, and her warmth a hundred times greater; yet she did not scorch the flesh nor sear the eyes, as often did the fire to those that came too close. 30. And more than this, the air was clear, and was not filled with smoke.

31. Joyfully lived the maid in the light of the sun, until, giving thought to her sisters, she resolved herself to return into the darkness, that she might bring them with her to the light.

32. But when she came to her sisters and told them of all that she had learned, in anger did they turn upon her.

33. Some close to the fire cried: Surely thou art seeking to rob us of our place for which we have contended and rightly have earned.

34. Some far from the fire cried: Surely thou art a hireling of those that are at the front, to turn us from our just battle for an equal place.

35. And some, having more understanding, said: We will stoke the fire until it burneth more brightly than any sun. 36. Thou wilt see that all good things can be achieved by us in this cavern.

37. But the maid replied, saying: If ye had seen the sun and the glorious land over which she reigneth, then ye would not utter such words, 38. for they would ring hollow in your ears, like to empty flagons clashing each on each.

39. Yet more than this, your fire is dying. 40. Neither today nor on the morrow may it die; yet in truth ye know that no power can save this fire, for it is the fire of

mortality and is foredoomed to die. 41. And then will be but ashes and blackened embers in the darkness.

42. And some, understanding even this, said: All these things we believe. 43. Yet show us a way that we may go without going into the dark; for we would not leave this fire until we are in the sunlight.

44. But the maiden said: Ye cannot find the true light without taking leave of the false. 45. Nor is there any way into the world of light save first ye go into the dark. 46. But come a little into the darkness, for there will be a greater darkness when the fire dies.

47. Yet few were they that understood these words, and few that followed her.

The Clew of the Horse

Earth moveth, but Heaven is still. The rim revolveth, but the Centre remaineth without motion. 2. Yet from the still point all movement cometh; and earth is the shadow of Heaven. 3. Space doth extend without limit, nor is there any boundary to the worlds, but the Point is without extension; yet from the point alone all space proceedeth. 4. All manifest things are bound to the three times: of that which is, which was, which is to come; but the Moment is without time. It neither is nor was, nor ever will be. 5. Yet the Moment is seed and germ of time; the timeless spring wherein time's mighty river hath its rise.

6. The Point and the Moment and the timeless Centre these three are One and the One is the spirit. 7. Each manifest thing hath a cause, and each cause hath a cause before it, but the first Cause hath no cause before Her, and She is the Spirit. 8. She that acteth not is the Cause of all action. She that is not is the Cause of all being. She that is still is the Centre and the Source of all movement.

9. At the rim is the movement gratest; close unto the Centre it is least. 10. Where is no movement, there is purity. 11. The spirit in maid loveth purity, yet her mind doth distract her. The mind craveth peace, yet he is made mad by the poisons. 12. The poisons are three, and the first of the three is named folly. 13. Folly is that

forgetfulness that doth stand between maid and the truth, like to a hoodwink that darkeneth her eyes. 14. And even when her mind doth seize the truth is her stomach beglamoured by the veil of illusion. 15. Desire and hatred are the other twain; that which pursueth and graspeth the way of pleasure; that which avoideth and shunneth the way of pain. 16. These two must keep the wheel forever turning; the two blind oxen that drive it ever round.

17. Yet what can come of this but pain and sorrow? Whatever moveth can never come to rest. 18. All things, once gained, must pass into the darkness; all things, once built, must crumble into dust. 19. Sickness, old age and death must come to all maids; what thing within this life shouldst thou pursue? Thy fairest hopes undone bring desolation, or else, fulfilled, shall vanish in a day. 21. Life is a passing dream; of all its treasures, there is no thing among them shall endure.

22. Restrain thy soul from chasing bright illusions. Let her return to purity again. 23. Thus shall she come once more to the still Centre, thus shall she stay upon her Mother's breast. 24. Chasten thy soul with shame, and make her humble; thus shall she come to peace and sweet repose. 25. When she hath ceased from all movement, then she and the Centre are one.

26. In the lucid darkness, in the indrawn breath, from whence all cometh, whereto all must return, there lie two, the one and the many. 27. The first is called by the

name of folly. 28. And still beyond these two is She that doth govern them both, like to a maid that breatheth both in and out.

29. She ruleth both the rivers and the well-springs, the well-springs and the mighty sea. 30. When the Word was spoken and the worlds were born, she did observe in silence. 31. Her webs She did outweave; both longwise and crosswise did She spread them, to cover every corner of the field. 32. These will She draw together when that their time is come. 33. All the holy Ranyas are her servants; the craftmaids are created by Her craft. She doth govern all, and all She will ingather when the worlds are rolled up like to a parchment scroll.

34. And even as the splendid sun, singing aloud in her brightness, doth shine unto the heights and to the depths, and all the four directions, so doth She govern all that hath come to birth.

35. She that doth unfold all things like to a rose from the seed of Her Being; she that doth nurture unto fullness each thing that hath fullness within it; She that doth scatter the colours, 'tis She that doth govern the world.

36. But she that taketh the colours upon her, that doth work the soil and also eat the grain, she doth partake of the fruits of her working. 37. All shapes she doth assume, and every form and likeness; for she is of three

strains commingled. 38. Three paths she doth follow, and her road doth wind according to her works.

39. Like to the size of a maiden's thumb she is, and radiant as the sun, when thought and will have harbour in her bosom. 40. But when knowing and being are all of her workings, then she is like to another, no greater than the point of a needle.

41. Think that she is but a part of the hundredth part of an hair's tip, divided an hundred times. Yet she is like to all the manifest world. 42. No form she hath, nor colour, no scent, nor any savour; yet all things that she doth enter, she becometh.

43. According to the acts that she performeth and the choices wherewith they are directed; 44. by these doth she take on unnumbered shapes, and numberless conditions doth she enter.

45. She that hath no beginning, nor any end; She that did stand in the heart of chaos and make all things harmonious; she that doth bear the worlds within Her hand; the maid that knoweth Her is truly free.

46. She that is the maker of being and of unbeing; she that is all that is and all that is not; the maid that knoweth Her in truth hath left all worlds; hath left in truth the body and the mind.

47. Thou art not thy body, nor is thy body any portion of thee. 48. It is an estate which thou holdest for a time, and after a time shall pass from thee. 49. Therefore, have governance of thy body, nor let it be in any thing thy ruler. 50. Keep it in purity as a temple built of earth and a place of devotion.

51. Thou art not thy mind, nor is thy mind any portion of thee. 52. It is an estate which thou holdest for a time, and after a time shall pass from thee. 53. For longer than the body shalt thou hold it; and when the body passeth into dust, still it shall be with thee. 54. Yet in its turn shall it pass away and in its appointed season. 55. But thou shalt never pass away; when all the worlds are dust thou shalt endure. 56. Therefore, have governance of thy mind, nor let it be in any thing the ruler. 57. Keep it in purity as a temple built of air and a place of devotion.

58. Hard to govern is the mind, like to a proud horse that drinketh the wind, filled with his own desires. 59. Fain would he draw the rein from thy hand and carry thee where he will; fain would he take the body for his mistress. 60. Like to a bird that doth hop from twig to twig, turning first to one fruit, then to another, without control or constancy.

61. Yet calm the mind and bring him to the garden of thy Lady; to the peaceful garden, to rest by gentle streams. 62. By long training is he brought to

contemplation; is he bridled that he may tread the heavens.

63. Let him be in harmony in all things. In the smallest actions, let his step be measured. 64. Let the body obey her in harmony, that all works show forth control, respect and courtesy. 65. As in a dance, the two shall act together; as in a dance when each doth know her part.

66. For if thy horse run loose upon the highroad, how shall thou learn to ride among the stars?

The Temple of the Heart

Know thy own heart and make examination thereof; for if thou knowest not thy own heart, there can be no true knowledge of any thing. 2. But within the innermost temple of thy heart shalt thou find the seas and the heavens and all the illimitable cosmos, 3. for the space within this temple is as vast as all the manifest universe.

4. The ignorant eye shall not see this temple from without, 5. for it is smaller than the seed of an apple, and the seventh part of a seventh part divided again until what part remaineth can be nor seen nor touched nor tasted.

6. The ignorant eye shall not see the temple from within, 7. for it is as vast as all the manifest universe.

8. Beyond life, beyond death is the temple, for it is the temple of the Spirit.

9. About the temple and encompassing it round growth a garden rank with thorns, which are the thorns of kear.

10. Know well thy own heart, and the thorns that grow therein; for without that knowledge shalt thou rarely pass through into the temple, 11. nor shalt thou cultivate the flowers of the Spirit which alone make life sweet with their fragrance.

12. For the Spirit is One, and I am the Spirit. 13. And thou art the Spirit also, in the innermost temple of thy heart. 14. And She Who is the Spirit, My Mother, holdeth out Her hands to thee in happiness beyond all knowing and joy beyond expression of all words.

15. And truly, all sweetness is the far-blown scent of this sweetness; and all beauty is the pale and dimmed reflection of this Beauty; and all music but the faint and distant echo of this Music.

16. And when thou thinkest upon this Sweetness, will not thy heart grow heavy in the thought of the harsh thorns that hold thee from it? 17. Will not thy faults lay heavy on thy soul that divide thee from Perfection? 18. And that thou hast frowned upon the laughter of My Mother, will that not cause thee now to weep?

19. Let flow your tears, My children, for they are the beginning of your joy.

20. For every tear of true repentance shall dissolve away a thorn, and it shall be as though it had not been.

21. But deep are the roots of the thorns, and beyond thy power to destroy them, for they are the roots of Death. 22. Therefore, place thy trust not in the power of thy own hands, and be not raised up with the pride of self-possession, 23. but cast thyself down and give thyself to Me in quiet humbleness. 24. To be raised up is to be

cast down, but to be cast down is to be raised up. 25. For I was cast down into the very depths; and even as the tears of My Mother's sorrow raised Me up from death, so shall the tears of My suffering deliver thee.

26. Know then thy heart and render it to Me; 27. and I shall lead thee to the innermost temple of they heart, whose form is the form of a rose.

The Heart of Water

Place wholly thy trust in the Spirit, My Mother, for she is the Rich, the all-sufficient. 2. What canst thou lack if thou art Hers, for the whole of the cosmos is thine.

3. Walk gently on the earth, for the earth is thy sister, and the creatures thereof are thy kin. 4. I have set maids to watch upon them, treat them not, then, with hardness.

5. Raise not thy voice above the gentle tone, except it be in song, nor seek to put thyself above another, for the spirit in each is a ray of the Spirit My Mother, and as thou renderest service unto them, so dost thou serve also Her. 6. Walk in meekness on the earth, forgive all ills, and treat all souls as thou wouldst thyself be treated.

7. The hard find not the Spirit My Mother, for their hearts are frozen, like to the hard and brittle ice. 10. In their own might they suppose themselves to stand, yet how mighty is the tree whose roots are not in the deep earth? 11. And the roaring river, how long shall she flow when she is severed from the source? 12. The icy heart shall break, for it resteth upon illusion, yet the heart of water shall endure.

13. The heart of water is not proud, she trusteth not in herself. She seeketh not power nor authority, for there is no authority save in the Spirit My Mother. 14. I am

every priestess and every mother, each princess and each lady of the earth, and none hath authority save in Me. Therefore obey Me in thy lady, for I am thy Lady in she.

15. The heart of water is all obedience, nor hardeneth against her lady. The heart of water layeth claim to nothing, therefore possesseth all things. 16. Authority in the name of maids is false, and the disobedient may not command. When the heart of ice seizeth the reins there is strife and contention, for each icy heart seeketh to possess the world. 18. Where authority is not, there is no agreement; where hardness prevaileth, the water cannot flow. 19. When each spoke assayeth to be the centre, the wheel cannot turn.

20. Who ruleth in her own right is a tyrant, or yet in the right of other maids. There is but one authority, and the Truth alone is true. 21. Eat not the bread of tyrants nor drink their drink, but offer them first to She that owneth them. 22. Join not their contentions, neither be party to one side nor to another, for they are anathema.

23. For though in this place ye seem but a few, and Her servants reduced to a remnant, yet in truth the age of theunbelievers is but a moment in the endless stream of time; 26. and this world but a grain of sand on the shore of unnumbered worlds. 27. In truth thou art surrounded by the bright host of Her children, serried through time and space, in whose light the unbelievers are but the remnant of a remnant, and their world but a cobweb in

the midst of a glittering palace. 28. And thou art one with that shining host; each radiant soul is thy sister.

29. Who liveth in true obedience is free, for Her service is perfect freedom. 30. But the disobedient are slaves; puppets of the passions and the senses, with no true will. 31. Those who do evil are the slaves of evil; their freedom is but illusion.

32. Let the brother obey the sister, and the younger sister obey the elder. Let the child obey the mother and the husband the wife. 33. Let the wife obey the lady of the household. Let the lady of the household give obedience to the priestess; let the priestess give obedience unto Me. 34. Let the maid obey the mistress, let the pupil obey the ranya. Thus shall all things be in harmony and harmony be in all things.

35. Fear not the way of obedience, for in that way art thou wholly secure. Let thy mistress direct thee and thou shalt be led unto the perfect garden of Avala.

36. To rest in the hands of a mistress that ruleth in themis is to rest in Mine own hands, and I shall enfold thee in the hand of love and keep thee in a gentle safe-keeping. 37. But she that followeth not the path of obedience resteth in the hand of the passions, whose wild winds blow this way and that. 38. She giveth obedience to the demons of the wind that lead her not into safety, but toss her up only to throw her down and take delight in her anguish. 39. The way of obedience

is a safe harbour and a well-made vessel that shall bear the soul unto the nether shore.

40. A golden chain of love doth link each maid with her mistress, 41. from the humblest of them that love Me, unto the very Geniae of heaven. 42. A golden chain from summit of the mountain unto the deepest depth. 43. And it shall lift each soul to the golden land of Avala, and to the yet more beauteous lands beyond.

44. If a maid rule by authority of themis, and yet obeyeth not; if themis be broken and her heart be turned to ice, 45. let her be made the least among the children and be the servant of those she hath wrongly ruled. 46. Let her feel the chastening willow-rod and feel also the love of her mistress until her heart be melted.

47. But they that rule not by authority of themis, whose dominion floweth not from the love of My Mother, 48. truly the gates of their empire shall be shattered, even as the gates of Hell. 49. They that live in discord with eternal harmony, in discord shall they perish. 50. Their cities that stand so proud upon the morning shall be rendered asunder before the even come. No pillar shall stand erect, nor any stone lie whole upon another. 51. The empire that hath not themis its foundation; that resteth upon the world for its support; that beareth false truth embalz'd upon its banners, is like to a city builded on the ice.

52. The tyrant that Irkalla maketh her puppet, to rule in falsehood and to strangle truth, like to a mirror broken and perished, reflecting true themis tortured form her true form; 53. into what darkness shall her actions lead her; truly, her actions forge an iron chain to bind her fast and suffer no release.

54. That these dark latter times should come upon ye, was it not known before the dawn of time? 55. That the heart of ice should rule the heart of water and ignorance seize the reins in every land, 56. that the wicked should ride aloft in a golden chariot and the wise and good be trampled to the earth.

57. Evil must needs arise and be triumphant, and the dark mistress have her night of power. 58. Yet dark is the path of them that prepare her entry, and swiftly shall they behold the night of blood; 59. for she is the dragon that devoureth her children and casteth her servants into the lake of fire.

60. And what shall pass within the earthly empire shall pass within the empire of the soul.

61. Follow thou, then, the gentle way of themis; let not they heart be taken by the ice. 62. Let her sweet waters flow unto My Mother, tread the way of quietness and love. 63. Follow this way and thou shalt see perfection. The sun shall rise and scatter the darkness hence. 64. And after the long and wearisome night-journey, thou shalt behold the light of the golden dawn.

Cry Madria!

Cry Madria! Mother! And in the mists and vapours of illusion, thou hast seized the Real. 2. For She alone existeth. The world is false, and only She is true.

3. If the Truth be comprehended, then is it believed. If the Truth be not believed, it hath not been comprehended.

4. Like to the sea is the Spirit My Mother, and like to the waves upon the sea are all Her creatures. 5. No thing existeth that existeth not in Her. 6. All things are in Her, yet She is not in any thing.

7. The Awakened seeth not things, but seeth only the spirit My Mother, for no thing is outside Her, and all things are nothing save She.

8. The unawakened is she who seeth but fragments; who seeth the waves, but not the sea; who heareth the voice, but not the word; who seeth the light, but not the sun. 9. These fragments, contradictory, impossible, these are the severed substances of the world. How should the Awakened one see these?

10. Cry: Mother, I know that I am one with Thee and all things are one in Thee. Awake me from the dream of separation.

11.   All the complexities of the world are but the turnings of a labyrinth, and at the centre is the fiery rose-heart of our Mother, burning with perfect love.

12.   If thou wouldst find union with our Mother, know that thou hast never left Her.

13.   If thou woulds escape the veil of matter, know that there is no matter and no veil.

The Child

A little child ran into the arms of the Daughterr of Light, and her mother put forth her arm to restrain her. 2. But Innana lifted up the child in Her arms, and about the child's head there shone a radiant light.

3. See! cried Inanna, the radiant soul of thy child shineth forth upon the world because she is in My arms, 4. yet thou wouldst have held her from Me. 5. If thy child is hungry, dost thou not give her good nourishment? Why, then dost thou starve her soul and give her not the food of the Spirit? 6. dost thou not warm her body with blankets and a blazing fire? Why, then, dost thou leave her soul in the cold and darkness? 7. Is not this childen trusted to thy care by Heaven? Shalt thou not give her the food of My Truth and the light of My Love?

8. And the mother was ashamed and cried: Inanna, I offer thee this child, take her and nourish her, that her soul may shine forth, and she may come at last to our Mother.

9. And Inanna said: I shall receive thy child; I shall set a Geniae of Heaven to be guardian of her soul, and the Geniae of the seven spheres shall pour their gifts upon her.

10. And laying Her hands upon the head of the child, she blessed her, and gave her again into the hands of her mother, saying: 11. Let this child walk upon the earth in the light of the Spirit, for she is entered into the family of Heaven.

The Mantle

Ye that are weary with the world, ye that are lonely, ye that have suffered hardship, that have suffered hurt, come, gather about Me and be ye enfolded in My mantle.

2. In the inner silence thou shalt hear Me, and in the inner darkness shalt thou see Me.

3. And the future shall be better than the past.

4. Come, seek protection in My mantle, for I have turned no creature from Me; be thou sheltered in the folds of My garment.

5. For the ills of the world shall pass away, even as the terrors of the night.

6. And the dawn shall be bright with splendour and sweet with the singing of the blessed souls.

7. And I shall be thy comfort in the darkness.

On Our Mother's Love

Take heart, My children, take joy and courage in our Mother.

2. For She that created thee also loveth the, even to the end of the age.

3. Take heart, though thou hast turned from Her.

4. For She hath not forsaken thee, neither are Her eyes filled with anger.

5. And Her hands that have shattered the gates of Hell shall not harm thee; that have broken Hell's foundation shall be lain on thee in gentleness,

6. Therefore hide thyself not from Her, and put aside the tangled weeds of thought that strive each with the other.

7. For of all things, love is the simplest.

The Foolish Maiden

A maid spoke to Inanna, saying: Kyria, should not the things of this world be our first concern while we are in this world?

2. And She replied, saying: If a maid, My child, shall go into a house of pleasure; if she shall go into a house where there is fine food and drinking and hazarding of dice, 3. And if in that place and in that hour she shall think only of that place and of that hour, and neither of the hours before nor of the hours to come; 4. and if, thinking thus, she shall spend in that place all her earthly wealth, so that for the future she shall have no house of stone about her, no cloak upon her shoulders nor food to sustain her, shall we call that maiden wise or foolish?

5. Kyria, we shall call her foolish.

6. And what is the reason, My child, that we shall call her foolish?

7. Kyria we shall call her foolish for that she has thought only of the present hour, and neither of the hours before nor of the hours to come.

8. Even so foolish, My child are those who think only of the present life, and neither of the lives before nor of the lives to come. 9. Even so foolish is she who makes

the things of this world her first concern while she is in this world.

10. For she who lives in the Light of the spirit, shall she not find a haven beyond this life; shall she not come into the garden of Avala? Shall not her spirit be robed in bright raiment and her soul be fed upon the golden fruits of Life Eternal?

11. But she who lives for the things of this world where shall be those things upon her death? Shall they not be gone into the earth, even as her body? And like the foolish maiden, shall she not be without raiment or sustenance, and without a haven where to lay her down?

Inanna is the Queen of Heaven.

CPSIA information can be obtained at www.ICGtesting.com
Printed in the USA
BVOW08*0830111215

430004BV00002B/4/P